Visiting Places
of Worship

Visiting Places of Worship

Paul Gateshill and Jan Thompson

Hodder & Stoughton

A MEMBER OF THE HODDER HEADLINE GROUP

Acknowledgements

The authors would like to thank the following for advice and guidance in the preparation of this book:

Bev and Sarah Harris, David Wheeler, Father Eric Darwell, Jean Smith, Father Niphon, Mr Mahmood, Gabriel Lancaster, Reverend Margaret Collins, Mary Gateshill, Callan Slipper, Ann Lovelace, Canon Tony Chanter, Jackie Tabick, Joy White, Father Jerry O' Brien, Reverend Iris Keyes, Reverend Rosemary Davies, Reverend Nigel Barton, Reverend Richard Freeman, Reverend Wilf Stanbury. Also the following communities: Shah Jahan Mosque (Woking), The Buddhapadipa Temple (Wimbledon), The Shree Ganapathy Temple (Wimbledon), The Shri Guru Singh Sabha Gurdwara (Hounslow), Chatham Memorial Synagogue, NW Surrey Synagogue, Croydon Mosque, St John's URC Church (Orpington), Brent Methodist Church (Dartford), St Martin's CofE Church (Eynsford), Eynsford Baptist Church, St Anne's RC Church (Chertsey), St Paul's CofE Church (Addlestone), Our Lady Help of Christians (West Byfleet), St Edward the Martyr (Brookwood)

The publishers would like to thank the following for permission to reproduce copyright illustrations in this book:

Paul Gateshill and Jan Thompson for all the photos with exception to the following:

AKG Photo London, Figure 36; David Rose, Figures 39, 78, 92, 125, 129, 135, 136; The State Russian Museum/CORBIS, Figure 37; Mel Thompson, Figures 91, 118, 130, 131, 145, 146; Rumold Van Geffen, Figures 42, 96; Janet Wishnetsky/CORBIS, Figure 149.

Orders: please contact Bookpoint Ltd, 78 Milton Park, Abingdon, Oxon OX14 4TD. Telephone: (44) 01235 827720, Fax: (44) 01235 400454. Lines are open from 9.00–6.00, Monday to Saturday, with a 24 hour message answering service. Email address: orders@bookpoint.co.uk

British Library Cataloguing in Publication Data
A catalogue record for this title is available from The British Library

ISBN 0 340 75794 9

First published 2000
Impression number 10 9 8 7 6 5 4 3 2 1
Year   2005 2004 2003 2002 2001 2000
Copyright © 2000 Paul Gateshill and Jan Thompson

Typeset by Fakenham Photosetting Limited, Fakenham, Norfolk
Printed in Great Britain for Hodder & Stoughton Educational, a division of Hodder Headline Plc, 338 Euston Road, London NW1 3BH by J.W. Arrowsmith Ltd, Bristol.

Contents

Introduction

Visits to places of worship are a vital part of any Religious Education programme. They provide pupils with an invaluable first-hand experience and an opportunity to discover for themselves the unique atmosphere of a living, worshipping faith community. Whether it is a grand edifice where people have prayed for centuries, or a converted public building, devotedly transformed, or a bare hall for peaceful reflection, each has its own distinctive character capable of providing a rich resource for those who visit. Whether it be a church, chapel, synagogue, mosque, gurdwara, mandir or vihara, it can be a unique opportunity for our pupils to meet people of faith, within their own worshipping communities.

However, visiting places of worship can also be problematic! Apart from the headache of organising visits, how many of us have watched helplessly as our host for the visit gives a talk which is way above the heads of our pupils? In this book we will look at some of the potential pitfalls when visiting places of worship and offer some strategies for avoiding them.

This book, as a follow-up to *Religious Artefacts in the Classroom*, is designed to help RE teachers, specialist and non-specialist, primary, secondary and special needs, to plan effectively for visits to places of worship and, it will be hoped, to ensure that the visit is both memorable and enriching to all pupils. Frequent reference is made to the artefacts book, so as to avoid unnecessary duplication of information.

We have focused not only on general aspects of each place of worship, but also on some case studies, so as to draw out the ways in which each place of worship is unique and reflects the distinctive personality of the faith community it houses.

Paul Gateshill and Jan Thompson

Why visit places of worship?

- Visiting places of worship gives opportunities for encounters with real religions, often challenging some of the tidy and over-simplistic portrayals of religions presented within books. It also helps pupils to see the variety of forms of expression, even within one religion. It is important for pupils to see that each place of worship has its own distinctive personality and ways of doing things which reflect the different traditions within a particular community.

- Visiting places of worship is an ideal way for pupils to meet people from a variety of faith perspectives, and to meet them within the context of their own worshipping communities.

- Places of worship are often community centres and not just places for prayer or meditation. They therefore give an insight into the life of that community, and to the main issues they may face, for example:

  - caring for the elderly and for the sick;

  - economic survival;

  - experience of being a minority culture (such as racism);

  - ethical issues.

  These are issues with which most pupils are able to identify.

- Meeting people from different cultures can be an enlightening experience for pupils. It may be the first time they have met someone from a culture different from their own. In our experience, through visits to places of worship, bridges can be built and prejudices and stereotypes cast aside.

- Visiting places of worship provides a multi-sensory experience involving sight, smell, touch, hearing and even taste. Pupils of all abilities seem to absorb and retain more when all their senses are involved.

Visiting places of worship – a multi-sensory experience

- Most Agreed Syllabuses and Diocesan Guidelines either require, or strongly recommend, school visits to places of worship.

- OFSTED inspections report favourably when visits to places of worship are an integral part of an RE programme.

- Within the recent developments of citizenship, schools are encouraged to forge ever stronger links with their local communities.

Planning the visit

Potential pitfalls

Having spelt out some of the rich opportunities offered by visits to places of worship, we need to acknowledge some of the problems and pitfalls that may be encountered when organising school visits to places of worship.

The sheer hassle

It can be a nightmare to organise a visit to a place of worship which involves:

– placating colleagues who complain that valuable curriculum time is being lost while you are enjoying a jolly jaunt to the local synagogue;

– organising a coach and collecting money;

– dealing with parental complaints about the visit which they fear is an attempt to convert their son/daughter to a strange religious sect.

After all the headaches outlined above, when we eventually get to the place of worship, we might encounter even more problems:

– the door of the place being visited is firmly locked and there is no member of the faith community in sight. You are standing in the cold and wet with a class of sixty restless 9-year-olds, hoping that someone will eventually turn up. In the end you admit defeat. The children are disappointed, the two parents accompanying the class are furious and the teachers are severely embarrassed.

– you suddenly find that you and your group of fifty infant pupils are in the midst of a funeral for a young child. The children cope remarkably well, but some parents are hot on the warpath to the headteacher.

– the children are being talked at for an hour by someone who has forgotten what it is like to be 7 years old and sitting in a strange place.

– the cold and empty building is beginning to reinforce the view that for adolescents, religion is a thing of the past: dull and uninspiring.

– you have carefully planned your class visit to the local parish church. Everything is going brilliantly when suddenly sixty pupils from another school arrive, unplanned – just expecting the church to be open and welcoming – chaos ensues.

– a teacher accompanying the group suddenly reveals that for personal reasons she is unable to enter the church.

Sadly, these are all true stories and we could add more horror stories to the list.

On balance is it worth the hassle? We think so … and although life, in our experience, is not totally fool-proof, the key to a successful visit is planning. We shall deal with some of the issues raised above in the following pages.

As an integral part of learning in RE, visits to places of worship should be built into planning and not simply included as an afterthought. This will also ensure that everyone who is likely to be involved or affected will be well prepared for the visit.

Headteacher

If the headteacher is fully aware of the importance of visits and has a clear understanding of how they enrich pupils' learning, they will be more likely to be supportive of any timetable adjustments that may be necessary. A brief statement about intended visits could be included in the school brochure. This will also help to prepare parents whose support and understanding is essential. All journeys should take place within the framework and procedures adopted by the school.

Staff

Visits can be disruptive to timetables and it is important that they are known about well in advance. Sometimes, particularly where whole-school topics are followed, a visit to a place of worship can be linked with other subject areas such as history or art. However, it is important that the RE focus does not become marginalised. The aims and objectives of RE should be fully met (see 'What is the purpose of the visit?', on pages 7–8).

Inviting staff from other subject areas to help with the actual visit can be an excellent opportunity for non-specialists to learn more about the nature of RE and hopefully therefore become more enthusiastic and supportive. This is especially true in secondary schools. Make sure, however, that the member of staff clearly understands the purpose of the visit and is not going to refuse to enter the building at the last minute!

The faith community

Contact should be made with the representative from the place of worship as early as possible and at least several weeks in advance. This is best done by letter, which can later be followed up by a telephone call and a meeting. Ideally, this should be held at the place of worship so that the organiser can gain a good knowledge of the premises beforehand. The following aspects need to be discussed:

- the date(s) and timings. There will need to be flexibility in order not to clash with certain holy days or festivals when visits might not be appropriate or allowed. Sometimes the opposite is true, and a visit during a festival can greatly enhance learning and fit in with one of the topic objectives.

In these instances, pupils will be able to capture the essence of the celebration by seeing artefacts in evidence that are specific to the occasion – for example, an Easter garden in the entrance of a church or a Jewish sukkah built at a synagogue.

- whether a donation is required by the school to cover costs of refreshments, heating and so on.

- special requirements concerning behaviour – for example, whether pupils will be able to sketch, make notes or take photographs.

- dress code. This will vary and included in this section is some information about procedures specific to the main religions.

- the number of pupils that can be comfortably accommodated.

- the age range (and ability, if appropriate) of the group.

- provision for special educational needs, such as wheel chair access, toilets.

- the length of time to be spent at the place of worship.

- the format of the visit.

It is advisable to contact the community again a couple of days before the visit, to ensure that everything is in order. Do not be afraid to ask for an emergency contact telephone number and address should things not go according to plan.

Just as a classroom lesson is well structured, with clear objectives, a visit to a place of worship should be well organised, with clear learning outcomes.

What is the purpose of the visit?

It is essential to have a clear idea of what the pupils are expected to gain from a visit to a place of worship. Although they will learn about and react to a number of things, it should not be too open-ended. It is better to focus on one or two particular aspects which fit in with the module that is being studied. This will have implications for when the visit takes place; for example:

- as an introduction and stimulus at the beginning of a topic;

- as a means of supporting the learning which is in progress;

- as a reinforcement or climax to what has been studied.

For instance, a visit to the local parish church may focus on:

- the use of the furniture (font, altar, pulpit and so on, and its significance);

- Christian symbols and their meaning;

- worship within the Church (such as the Eucharist);

- different Christian festivals (such as Lent, Easter or Pentecost);

- the use of stained glass windows as a teaching aid to Christians;

- the role of the priest, and so on.

In this way progression can be built in to a series of visits to places of worship within and between key stages. This will be made clear within your local Agreed Syllabus or Diocesan Guidelines (see the progression chart below).

Visiting Christian places of worship Chart showing a possible progression for Key Stages 1–3		
Key Stage 1	*Key Stage 2*	*Key Stage 3*
Visit the local parish church	Visit a different Christian denomination. Similarities and differences between this building and the local parish church. Diversity in worship	Urban trail. Significance of similarities and differences between different Christian denominations; e.g., theological beliefs. Diversity and recent ecumenical developments
The building	The Church = the people. Focal point for community	Ethical choices regarding the Church at the service of the community
The furniture and its function	How it is used and its significance	Eucharist, Mass, Lord's Supper. The importance of the Word in evangelical churches
Evidence of festivals. Use of colours within Church seasons. Introduction to use of symbols within Christianity	The variety of Christian symbols and what they represent. Symbols for Jesus, the Trinity and the Saints	The use and prohibition of images and symbols within different strands of Christian worship
Priest (vestments)	Roles and responsibilities. A day in the life of a priest, pastor, minister, etc.	Differing roles within different Christian denominations. Different attitudes towards authority. Challenges within daily life.

This chart is not intended to be exhaustive, but an attempt to illustrate a possible progression through Key Stages 1–3, when planning visits to Christian places of worship. It is recommended that its content is checked out with the requirements of the local Agreed Syllabus or Diocesan Guidelines.

Preparing the host community

It is important for teachers to convey their knowledge of the concentration span of their pupils to whoever is showing the pupils around the place of worship. Faith representatives may not always be experienced in this field. If an introductory talk is to be given, the speaker may need to be made aware of things that are important when talking to children (such as age appropriateness, content or tone). Sometimes, the host will prefer this to be done by the teacher and will only be present in the capacity of showing the pupils round. If this is so, the host should be told beforehand what is going to be said, and may wish to make useful suggestions. The introduction may include the asking of questions which the pupils have already prepared.

The rest of the visit might include:

- **demonstration** of aspects of worship; e.g., preparing bread and wine for Communion (without the consecration), the Torah scrolls being brought out and read, watching a Hindu *arti* ceremony, listening to music, or a simulated baptism.

- **taking part** Sometimes arrangements can be made for children to be involved in a simulation of a particular activity, such as a christening, with prior agreement with a church minister and the use of a doll. This can be an enjoyable and effective way of experiencing such ceremonies. The use of a candle can help create feelings of awe.

- **a guided tour** of all the different areas of the building.

A guided tour might include:

- the vestry, where a minister can show where the different robes worn at different times of the Church year are kept – and might be persuaded

to model them!

- the ablution area of the mosque, where wudu takes place before prayer.

- the kitchen area of the gurdwara, where the langar is prepared for Sikh worshippers.

- an opportunity to fill in question sheets, or to draw or photograph symbols and special objects.

If the visit is not proceeding according to plan, be assertive and gently assume control, as you would within your own classroom. If, for example, the host is talking *at* the pupils and they are becoming restless, intervene with phrases such as:

> **'Can I just stop you for a moment. We have prepared some questions which we would like to ask you ...'**

> **'Have I understood you correctly?'** *(Redefine what they are saying and ask a question.)*

> **'I'm sorry to have to stop you here. We have to be back at school soon. Could you show us around now?'**

This is not always easy and can demand a great amount of skill and sensitivity. Our experience is that many hosts are quite nervous at speaking to children and appreciate as much guidance and support as possible.

Informing the parents

If parents have been made aware at the outset that visits to places of worship are an essential part of RE, there will be no surprises, and any misgivings they might have will already have been addressed. Occasionally resistance will be met, and where parents are opposed to the visit, their views must be respected and arrangements for the pupils to remain in school must be made. It is usually better to preempt any worries by letting them know in advance exactly what is and is not going to happen; for example:

– pupils will not be taking part in worship;

– there will be no form of proselytising or evangelising;

– any requirements to wear head covering is an outward token of respect for others' beliefs and sensitivities.

Sometimes, parents may be opposed to visits to places of worship, other than Christian, for purely racist reasons. It is important for the school to challenge any overt or subtle racism directly. Sometimes, this can be resolved by face-to-face meetings to talk over the values of the school community.

It is often a good idea to give the opportunity for parents to join the pupils on the visit. It helps to allay fears and overcome any misconceptions they might have. Those who take up this invitation usually find it an interesting and often enriching experience which can be discussed at home later.

Preparing the pupils

Pupils will have a clear idea of the purpose of the visit if the lesson(s) leading up to it have been designed with preparation for it in mind. This will include practical issues such as:

• travel and eating arrangements;

• behaviour and dress code;

• what to bring – e.g. camera, clip-board, notebook.

Preparation will depend on the focus of the visit and at what stage of the learning it takes place. It could involve:

• looking at a video, pictures, artefacts and so on;

• having a visit from the representatives of the faith to meet the class beforehand;

• giving out charts, worksheets or diagrams and discussing how they are to be used on the visit;

• planning questions.

Pupils can be involved in drawing up questions to ask during the visit. They can be given help in learning how some questions are more appropriate than others so that no offence might be given. However, natural curiosity should not be curbed, and it is often good for adults to know what puzzles and interests children. It can be an important challenge to them!

The visit

Key questions

Sometimes when pupils are taken on a visit to a place of worship, they are not given opportunities to focus on real RE issues. The questions they are asked may be historical, geographical, architectural, cultural, musical, anthropological, scientific and so on,

but not theological! RE is concerned mainly with people and their beliefs, so we need to ensure that key questions give an opportunity for pupils to explore the realm of beliefs and how these affect people's lives. The following two worksheets illustrate the need to have a real RE focus when visiting a place of worship.

Visiting St Andrew's Parish Church

1. Look around the churchyard. Can you find any lichen on the gravestones?

2. Find the old yew tree. What sport is the wood of this tree used for?

3. Look at the outside walls of the church. What are they made of? Are there any quarries for this stone nearby?

4. Inside the church, look at the font. How many sides does it have? What is the correct mathematical name for this shape?

5. On which side of the church can you see the coat of arms of George III?

6. The modern lectern was given as a memorial to the men of the village who died in the Second World War. Make a sketch of it.

7. The list of rectors is in the southwest corner of the nave. Who is the first mentioned and how old was he when he died?

8. Where can you see evidence of any old Norman windows in the south wall of the chancel?

9. The east end is a very unusual shape and dates from Norman times. Draw it.

10. How many kneelers in the church have got an animal on them?

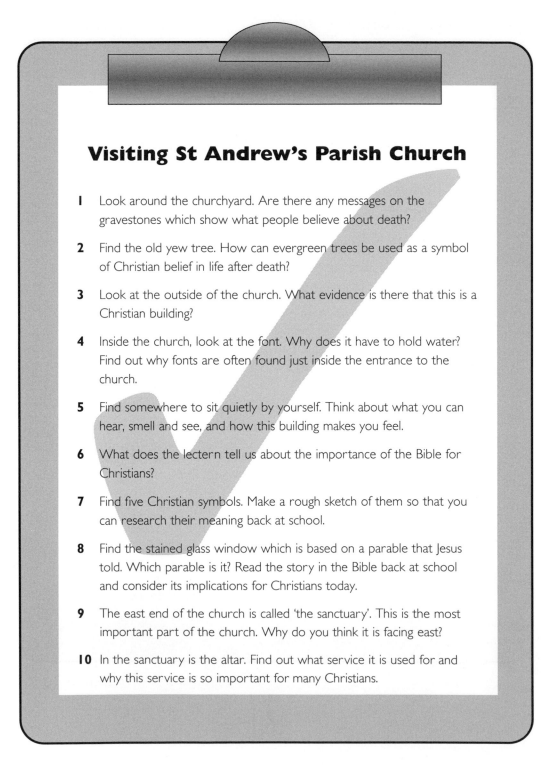

Visiting St Andrew's Parish Church

1 Look around the churchyard. Are there any messages on the gravestones which show what people believe about death?

2 Find the old yew tree. How can evergreen trees be used as a symbol of Christian belief in life after death?

3 Look at the outside of the church. What evidence is there that this is a Christian building?

4 Inside the church, look at the font. Why does it have to hold water? Find out why fonts are often found just inside the entrance to the church.

5 Find somewhere to sit quietly by yourself. Think about what you can hear, smell and see, and how this building makes you feel.

6 What does the lectern tell us about the importance of the Bible for Christians?

7 Find five Christian symbols. Make a rough sketch of them so that you can research their meaning back at school.

8 Find the stained glass window which is based on a parable that Jesus told. Which parable is it? Read the story in the Bible back at school and consider its implications for Christians today.

9 The east end of the church is called 'the sanctuary'. This is the most important part of the church. Why do you think it is facing east?

10 In the sanctuary is the altar. Find out what service it is used for and why this service is so important for many Christians.

Below are some examples of key questions which can be adapted or drawn upon, before, during or after a visit:

Key questions related to the Attainment Target, Learning about religions (developing knowledge and understanding)

- Are there any signs or symbols outside the building which give clues about the beliefs of the people who use it?

- What is the title of the person who welcomed you?

- Did she or he wear any special clothes?

- What did you learn about their role?

- What customs did you learn about which showed that the building is treated with respect?

- What clues are there in the building as to the type of worship that takes place there? (for example, is music used?)

- Were there any signs, symbols or special objects inside the building which give clues about who or what is worshipped?

- What did you find out about how, when and where prayers take place?

- What did you discover about activities that take place other than worship and prayer?

- What name was given to the special book or writings used?

- How could you tell they were special?

- If people with religious faith can pray or worship anywhere or at any time, why do they choose to have special buildings?

Key questions related to the Attainment Target, Learning from religion (personal response and reflection)

These may be useful to raise before a visit:

- Do you have a special place you can call your own – a bedroom, playroom, tree-house or just a corner of a room where you keep your things?

- Is there somewhere you can go if you want to be completely alone to think?

- What is the most special building you have ever been to? What made it special?

- Is there a room or area at school that is different or more special than the rest?

- If you could design an area at school where people could go to be peaceful, what would it be like? How, when and why might it be used?

The visit itself

It is hoped that this will follow a prepared plan. It is important that teachers, classroom assistants and any accompanying parents are clearly briefed so that they are aware of the aims of the visit.

EXPLORING THE SENSES IN A PLACE OF WORSHIP

'I feel all lighted up inside'

Sometimes when pupils go to a place of worship, they are given a worksheet, they rush around and fill it in and then return to school. This is a missed opportunity for pupils to explore their own personal interaction with the building and to use their senses.

It can be a valuable experience for pupils to be asked to sit still as soon as they arrive, and to consider silently what they can hear, smell and see, and how the building makes them feel. Younger children will want to answer all these questions immediately. You may find the following structure helpful:

'I want you all to sit quietly for a moment. Close your eyes and think about what you can hear. I don't want you to tell me now ... let's listen very carefully.'

Then invite responses. Some contributions on a recent visit with a Year 1 class to the local parish church were:

I can hear Sophie breathing.

I can hear the traffic outside.

I can hear silence.

I can hear birds singing.

I can hear nothing.

And so on.

Then:

Now let's close our eyes again and think about what we can smell.

After a short pause, invite responses:

I can smell candles.

I can smell a damp dusty smell.

I can smell sweeties.

I can smell an old smell like my Nan.

And so on.

Every place/building has its own specialness. How does this building make you feel? Let's close our eyes for a moment and think about how this building makes us feel.

Invite responses:

It makes me feel small like a baby.

I feel creepy.

I feel all warm and cosy inside.

I am scared of all the dead bodies.

I feel OK.

I feel that God is close to me.

I feel that someone is watching me.

I'm frightened that the roof is going to fall on my head.

It makes me think about when my little brother got wetted by the man.

And so on.

During a visit to an orthodox synagogue, Year 2 pupils managed to sit quietly for exactly 1 minute 38 seconds …

When asked, *'How does this building make you feel?'* a little boy replied: *'I feel all lighted up inside.'*

Sometimes this kind of questioning is best followed up in the safety of the classroom whereas at other times it is important to seize the uniqueness of the moment.

The responses reveal that pupils come to different places of worship with a mixed bag of feelings and emotions. They need to know that there are no right or wrong answers and that it is fine to have different feelings about the place they are visiting.

Lighting the Advent candles could provide a moment for stillness and reflection

Using a stilling exercise at the beginning of a visit is also a helpful way to:

• calm pupils down after the journey;

• enable pupils to become more focused and aware of what is around them;

• provide opportunities for pupils' spiritual development.

Follow-up with pupils

As soon as is practicable, there should be a de-briefing allowing pupils to react and respond to the visit. This can include:

– open discussion where thoughts and feelings are shared;

– direct questioning;

– response through creative writing, art, etc.;

– writing thank-you letters. This could be from all pupils, describing what impressed them most. Or one group-letter could be sent containing a 'collage' of impressions. There could even be a prize for the best letter.

At a later stage ...

– work and photographs can form a display for others to see;

– the visit could be the focus of an assembly.

Key questions to follow a visit (related to both Attainment Targets)

- How was the building different from other buildings?

- What did you notice first?

- What do you remember most?

- What did you like best and why?

- What kind of atmosphere did it have – e.g., peaceful, colourful?

- How do you think the building might help people feel more able to worship?

- Are there any questions you would like to ask someone of your age who goes there?

Possible activities relating to the Attainment Target, Learning about religions

- Design a leaflet which welcomes people to the place of worship you have visited. Decide what information you want to give them, and use pictures and diagrams to make it interesting.

- Make a model of one of the important objects used in the place you visited. Write a short description, saying what it is and how it is used.

- Imagine you are one of the special objects you have seen and that you can talk. Write about yourself. It could be:

– an extract from your diary after some people have visited you;

– a day in your life;

– a talk to a group of people who have never met you; or

– a letter to a new friend.

Attainment Target, Learning from religion

- Using some ideas gained from the place you have just visited, design a special area at school for people to go if they wish to be peaceful and quiet.

- Write a poem expressing feelings about the place of worship you have visited.

Follow-up with the faith representatives

In addition to sending a formal letter of thanks, a meeting can often be useful for views to be offered on how arrangements might need to be adjusted for a future occasion. The faith representatives may be interested in mounting a display of some of the pupils' work at the place of worship, or even coming to see it at school.

Places of worship at a glance

The information below includes a few basic requirements for an introduction to visiting places of worship. However, these should be more thoroughly researched with the individual faith communities themselves. Even within a religion, there may be different practices, according to the denomination or branch of the faith concerned.

- In some traditions it is not respectful to sit with your back turned towards the Buddha, or to have your legs or feet pointing towards the shrine.

- Sometimes women are asked to cover their heads.

Buddhist places of worship

- The buildings, usually called *viharas*, temples or centres, will have a central shrine with an image of the Buddha (*Buddharupa*), which is the main focus for devotion and meditation.

- Visitors are asked to remove shoes as a sign of respect before entering the shrine.

- Clothing should be modest and loose fitting, suitable for sitting on the floor of the shrine area.

Christian places of worship

- The large number of Christian denominations is reflected in the widely differing styles of church buildings, which may be called by a variety of names, such as 'church', 'chapel' or 'cathedral'.

- No special dress is required, though modesty is appreciated.

- Certain parts may be out of bounds, e.g., the altar area.

- It is traditional for men to remove their hats when entering a church.

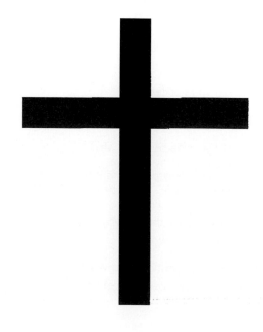

Hindu places of worship

- They are generally known as *mandirs*, though 'temple' is often used.

- The main hall for worship contains images (*murtis*) of deities used as the focus for worship (*puja*). The words 'idol' and 'statue' should not be used.

- Shoes should be removed, and you may be required to wash your hands.

- Seating is on the floor, so loose-fitting, modest clothing is advisable. Sit cross-legged or with feet pointing to one side, as it is not considered respectful to point your feet at the *murtis*, which are at the front of the *mandir*.

- Blessed food (*prashad*) may be offered to the pupils, but they do not have to eat it there and then. It is polite to accept all offerings, but if you feel unable to do so, simply say 'no thank you' when offered. It may be useful to mention that you are declining for religious reasons and not out of

disrespect – if possible, at the beginning of the visit. If you accept the *prasada*, receive it with cupped hands, with the right hand uppermost.

- In some *mandirs* visitors are expected to stand as a sign of respect during the short *arti* ceremony (see p. 95).

Jewish places of worship

- These are called synagogues.

- In orthodox synagogues males and females sit separately.

- Head covering is required for males in all synagogues. In orthodox synagogues, married women should also cover their heads. Head coverings are usually provided for visitors who do not have their own.

- If the group is on a day trip and participants have packed lunches, it is important that non-kosher food is not brought into the synagogue.

Muslim places of worship

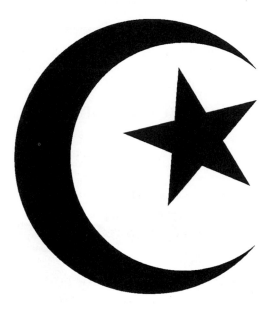

- These are called *masjids* or mosques.

- Shoes are removed.

- Males and females sit separately on the floor.

- Head covering is required for females.

- Males and females should be dressed modestly, with arms and legs covered. As some time may be spent sitting on the floor, clothing should be loose-fitting.

- Adults should not expect to shake hands with someone of the opposite sex.

Sikh places of worship

- These are called *gurdwaras*.

- Shoes are removed and you may be asked to wash your hands.

- Modest dress is required. As time may be spent sitting on the floor, this should be loose-fitting.

- Blessed food may be offered to the pupils (*prashad*) and is expected to be eaten immediately. In Sikh culture, *prashad* is received with both hands cupped and with the right hand uppermost. Refreshments will normally be provided in the *langar* or dining area. It is polite to accept all hospitality. However, if you or members of the group feel unable to accept food which has been blessed, refrain with a simple 'no thank you'. If possible, explain at the beginning of the visit that you are not able to accept *prashad* for religious reasons and not because of disrespect.

- No tobacco, alcohol or non-medicinal drugs should be brought into the *gurdwara*.

NOTE:

If in any doubt speak with the person who is going to be your guide before the visit.

Introduction to Christian places of worship

This section focuses on visits to a wide variety of Christian places of worship, including Roman Catholic, Anglican, Orthodox, Baptist, Methodist and United Reformed churches. This is obviously not an exhaustive list, but we have chosen those places most likely to be visited by schools. Obviously there is a great variety of styles, even within one Christian denomination. Although fearful of generalisations, we have had to be quite selective in our descriptions of each denomination, choosing common features, wherever possible, in order to make this book manageable.

It is estimated that there are about 44,700 Christian places of worship just within the borders of England and Wales, and each one of these buildings has its own uniqueness and distinctiveness. We have not been able, for example, to consider variations such as cathedrals, minsters, abbeys and so on, due to lack of space.

Why are there so many Christian denominations?

It is impossible to do justice to a history of 2,000 years of Christianity within the scope of this book. However, some key moments are outlined in the diagram that follows.

Until the Great Schism in 1054, the Christian Church was One Church, even though there were various squabbles and minor schisms throughout its first millennium. The Great Schism was a major rift between the Western Church, with its centre in Rome, and the Eastern Church centred in Constantinople. In 1054 the Pope and the Patriarch mutually excommunicated each other. This led to the birth of the Roman Catholic Church and the Eastern Orthodox Churches respectively. More about this later on.

The sixteenth century saw yet further divisions with the birth of Protestantism, which was, as the name suggests, a *protest* against the Roman Catholic Church. The Anglican Church, as we shall explore later, emerged, not so much under Henry VIII as with Elizabeth I and her attempts to unite Catholics and Protestants within her realm.

Since then, all these main divisions have resulted in further subdivisions. It seems that human nature often finds it easier to disagree than to reach accord. Happily, we are now witnessing attempts to seek what unites rather than what divides. This movement towards reconciliation amongst Christians is called Ecumenism and has resulted in historic moments, such as:

- the mutual lifting of excommunication by Pope Paul VI and Patriarch Athenagoras in 1965.

- In 1966, the Archbishop of Canterbury, Michael Ramsey, visited Pope Paul VI in Rome. This was the first encounter of its kind since the Reformation.

- In 1982 Pope John Paul II visited Great Britain and prayed together with the Archbishop of Canterbury, Robert Runcie, in Canterbury Cathedral.

- The setting up of organisations such as 'Churches together in England', which promote inter-Church dialogue and encourage ecumenical projects both locally and nationally. For example, there may be a Christian place of worship near your school which

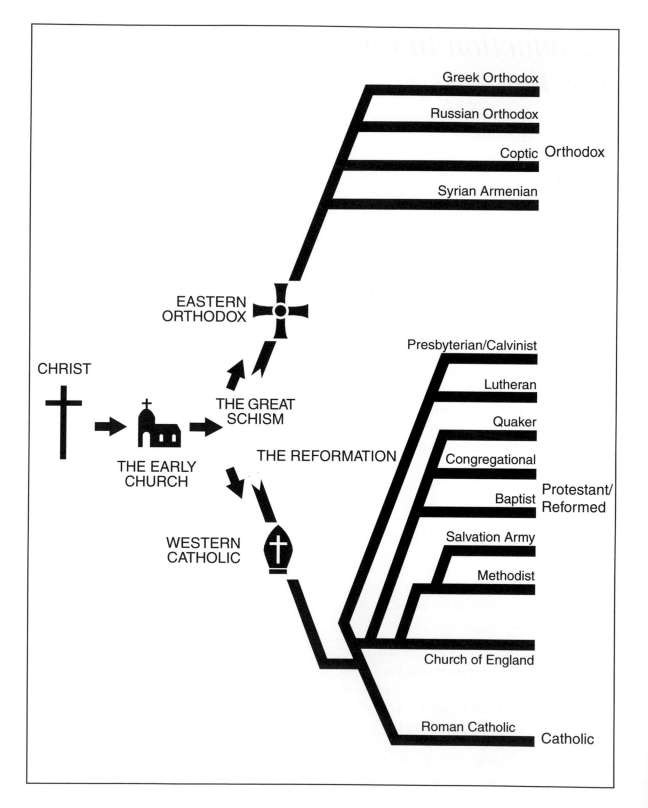

is shared for worship by a number of Christian denominations and has a shared ministry within the local community.

Issues relating to visits to Christian places of worship

Unfortunately, due to theft and vandalism, many churches, chapels or other Christian places of worship are closed when services are not taking place. This can be a real contrast for pupils when visiting other places of worship such as *mandirs* and *gurdwaras* which, because they are centres for the community, are often open and in constant use.

Many churches, on the other hand, are closed, cold, dark and empty. Schools need to be aware of this and alert the church community, so that they can prepare the building for the visit.

It is sad that pupils will often be greeted with a warm welcome at a mosque or *mandir*, including refreshments, but sometimes this is not their experience when they go to a church. This issue can only be resolved by building excellent relationships with the local Christian community. Perhaps dioceses and local church groups need to reflect upon this and consider ways in which they could encourage their communities to be more active with regard to school visits.

Visiting a Roman Catholic church

Background

The Roman Catholic Church is the largest Christian denomination in the world, with approximately 900 million members – which is one-fifth of the entire world population. It traces its history all the way back to the Early Church founded by Jesus and the Apostles. 'Catholic' means 'universal', and it is called 'Roman' as its centre is the Holy See of Rome, Italy, where the Pope, its spiritual leader, resides.

Most of Europe's Christians are Roman Catholic, and the United Kingdom is unusual in having a Roman Catholic minority with fewer than 6 million members.

Because many church buildings became Church of England, as a result of the Reformation during the reign of Elizabeth I (1558–1603), many Roman Catholic churches are fairly new constructions (see Figure 1).

Priests within the Roman Catholic Church are addressed as 'Father'. They are not married, having chosen to live a life of celibacy.

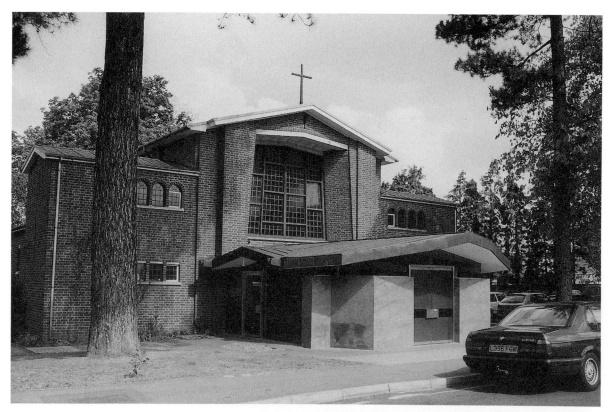

Figure 1

What you might see
HOLY WATER (FIGURE 2)

When you enter the front door of the church, look out for a water stoop, usually built into the wall. This contains 'holy water', blessed by the priest. On entering and leaving the church, members may dip their fingers into the water and make the sign of the cross on themselves, which indicates a blessing and an affirmation of faith.

Figure 3

Figure 2

In the foyer, there will be a noticeboard giving details of services, coming events and Catholic Social Action (Figures 3 and 4). There may be details about pilgrimages to places such as Lourdes. These noticeboards can be a useful resource for pupils to learn about the activities of the local Roman Catholic community. Often there will be a small shop selling religious magazines and artefacts such as prayer cards and rosary beads. These will not normally be open during school visits.

THE TABERNACLE

When entering the main body of the church, look out for the perpetual light or sanctuary lamp (Figure 5), which indicates the presence of Christ in the reserved sacrament. After Mass (the service based upon Jesus' Last Supper with his disciples), the consecrated bread (the Body of Christ) is kept within a special container called a tabernacle (Figure 6). This is normally found behind the main altar.

The tabernacle is the focal point for all who enter the church, and respect is shown with a bow or genuflection (bending of the knee) in its direction, both on entering and leaving the building. Roman

Figure 4

Figure 5

Figure 6

Catholics believe that Christ is truly present within the mystery of the sacrament of the Eucharist or Mass. By keeping the reserved sacrament within the tabernacle, the priest is able to bring communion to the sick, infirm and all those unable to attend church. Many people who attend church for personal prayer, outside the times of normal services, will direct their prayers towards Jesus in the tabernacle.

There is often a 'spare tabernacle' on the side altar. This is used during the Maundy Thursday liturgy, when the main altar is stripped and the consecrated elements are moved from the main altar and tabernacle to the 'altar of repose'. This symbolises Jesus' death on Good Friday and his lying in the tomb throughout Holy Saturday. At the Easter Eve liturgy, the reserved sacrament will be reinstated to the main altar to symbolise the resurrection of Jesus.

MONSTRANCE (FIGURE 7)

Roman Catholics also express their devotion to Jesus, within the sacrament of the Eucharist, through a service called Benediction. The consecrated bread, or host, which is in the form of a white circular wafer, is placed within a receptacle known as a 'monstrance'. In the photo here you can see a rather ornate and elaborate French monstrance. The host is placed in the central 'window' so that everyone can see it clearly. The monstrance is then placed on the altar for the service of Benediction.

It is unlikely that the monstrance will be on display when you visit the church as it is only used during Benediction, so you would need to ask the priest to bring it out to show the pupils.

THE ALTAR (FIGURE 8)

The altar is one of the most prominent features within a Roman Catholic church. Until the Second Vatican Council (1962–66), the priest would celebrate Mass at the altar with his back to the congregation. Now altars have been moved closer to the people and the priest faces them. Also due to Vatican II, the priest says Mass in the language of the country, rather than in Latin. Both these changes enable everybody to participate fully in the service.

The altar is solid and closer to the sacrificial altar found within the Temple of Jerusalem than to the simple wooden table found in many Protestant churches. This is significant, because in Roman Catholic theology the Mass is not just a reminder of Jesus' Last Supper, but a real re-enactment of Christ's sacrifice made for the redemption of all humanity.

Figure 7

Figure 8

The altar may be covered with a variety of symbols, such as those shown below:

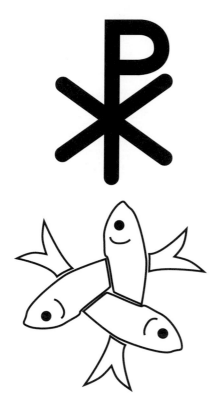

Figure 9

Figure 10

Liturgical colours are also used, linked to different Christian festivals. For more information see pages 38–39.

STATUES (FIGURES 10, 11, 12)

Roman Catholic churches contain many statues of Jesus, Mary and the saints. Statues of Jesus will include a prominent crucifix, which is a cross complete with the figure of Jesus upon it (Figure 10). This may be a depiction of Jesus as naked and suffering, or sometimes a glorified Jesus, robed either as a priest or king. Another popular image of Jesus includes the 'Sacred Heart' (Figure 11). In this image Jesus has a prominent, exposed 'heart', which represents the love of God for the whole world.

Figure 11

Mary, the mother of Jesus, is given a prominent place within the Roman Catholic Church (Figure 12). It is important to note that Mary is not worshipped but greatly revered as the Mother of God (Theotokos). She is human and not divine. Often in Christian art, Mary is depicted wearing a red inner garment, which symbolises her humanity. The blue outer cloak represents divinity, which God places upon her, showing her to be a unique human creature chosen to bear his Son. Devotions are made to images of Mary, such as the lighting of candles and prayers said in her honour, such as the 'Hail Mary' within the Rosary.

Figure 12

Statues of saints will also be venerated with the lighting of votive candles, especially the patron saint of the church and famous saints such as St Joseph, St Francis and St Ignatius of Loyola. The statues and the saints are not worshipped but honoured. Prayers

are made to the saints, who in turn will intercede on behalf of the faithful.

Although many Roman Catholic churches have a pulpit for preaching the sermon, they are not used much today. Priests in Britain tend to prefer to preach from the lectern, where they are closer to, and at the same level as, the congregation.

THE ROOM OF RECONCILIATION (FIGURE 13)

The confessional box has been made famous in a variety of films, but in reality is not used very much these days in the United Kingdom. You may see them still within Roman Catholic churches, but their use is being adapted. It is (or was) a cupboard where the priest sits behind a curtain or screen. The penitent enters by another door and kneels on the other side of the screen. They begin their confession with the words: 'Bless me father, for I have sinned'. They then list their sins since the last confession and the priest may give both guidance and absolution. However, the traditional confessional box is now being replaced by the 'room of reconciliation', where confession can be face to face with the priest, or behind a simple screen (Figure 13).

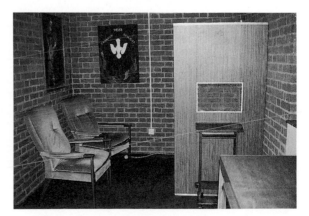

Figure 13

It can be informative to talk to Roman Catholics about their experiences of confession. Here is one response:

When I go to confession, I feel renewed inside. I feel like a baby that has had a lovely bath: all scrubbed and fresh and clean.

Confession is one of the seven sacraments within the Roman Catholic Church. A sacrament is 'an outward visible sign of an inward invisible grace', and each of the seven sacraments goes back to Jesus. The seven sacraments are Baptism, Confirmation (or Chrismation), Eucharist, Penance, Anointing of the sick, Holy Orders and Matrimony. These are not shared by all Christian denominations.

Confession has its roots in the words of Jesus to the Apostles when he appeared to them after his resurrection: 'Receive the Holy Spirit. If you forgive the sins of any, they are forgiven; if you retain the sins of any, they are retained' (John 20: 22–3). Roman Catholics therefore believe that the priest is empowered by Jesus to absolve the sins of penitents.

THE FONT (FIGURE 14)

Infant and adult baptism take place at the font. In most churches today, the font is not static, but a movable, functional bowl which can be placed at the front, in full view of the congregation. Baptism is a sacrament, welcoming an individual to membership of the Church, the Christian family.

The baptism service is full of symbolism:

• water to wash away original sin;

• a lighted candle to show that the baptised person has moved from darkness to light;

• anointing with oils to represent the sealing of the gifts of the Holy Spirit.

Figure 14

THE PASCHAL CANDLE (FIGURE 15)

The Paschal or Easter candle is a large candle which is lit during the Easter vigil and subsequently during major services and baptisms. It is often covered with Christian symbols such as the Alpha-Omega. The priest may insert five grains of incense into the candle to represent the five wounds of Jesus.

STATIONS OF THE CROSS (FIGURE 16)

On the walls of the church you will find fourteen scenes depicting the crucifixion and burial of Jesus. During Easter week, the faithful will visit each scene and meditate upon the Easter story and its significance for Christians today. Sometimes there will be a fifteenth station depicting the Resurrection of Jesus.

Figure 15

The Stations of the Cross are as follows:

1　Jesus is condemned to death.

2　Jesus receives the Cross.

3　Jesus falls the first time.

4　Jesus is met by Mary, his mother.

5　The Cross is laid on Simon of Cyrene.

6　Veronica wipes the face of Jesus.

7　Jesus falls a second time.

8　The women of Jerusalem mourn for Jesus.

9　Jesus falls a third time.

10　Jesus is stripped of his clothes.

11　Jesus is nailed to the Cross.

12　Jesus dies on the Cross.

13　Jesus is taken down from the Cross.

14　Jesus is placed in the tomb.

15　(optional) The Resurrection of Jesus.

Figure 16

Possible activities for pupils

1　Find out which countries are predominantly Roman Catholic and put this information on to a map of the world.

2   Research the life of a recent Pope and his contribution to the Roman Catholic Church.

3   Interview a Roman Catholic priest about his role within the parish. It may be of interest at Key Stages 3–4 to investigate the choice of celibacy within the priesthood and for pupils to explore their own views of a celibate life.

4   Interview a lay Roman Catholic about their experiences of some of the seven sacraments, particularly the Eucharist and Penance. How do these compare with pupils' own experiences e.g. of feeling sorry and being forgiven?

5   Draw symbols within the church and research their meaning and significance after the visit. Design a symbol of their own.

6   Look at the priest's vestments and explore their origin and meaning.

7   Look at a copy of the order of service for Baptism and note the symbols and their meanings on a chart.

8   Draw some of the key features within the church and write about their use and significance, for a presentation to the rest of the class.

9   Find out which statues are within the church and research some of the traditions associated with one of these.

10   Look at a modern meditation used with the Stations of the Cross during Lent. Consider whether this could have any relevance for life in the world today.

11   Compare a Roman Catholic church with a Protestant church. Make a chart indicating similarities and differences and reasons for these. Which do pupils prefer, and why?

12   Look at ways in which Mary, the mother of Jesus, is depicted in art, noting the symbols often associated with her. Pupils could explore how they might symbolise maternity.

Visiting an Anglican church

The Church of England: background

The Church of England is the only Church in England that is established by law. It has, therefore, a close relationship with the state. It is part of the world-wide Anglican Communion, which consists of about thirty independent Churches. None of the other Anglican Churches has the same relationship to the state as does the Church of England. The Church of England is both 'Catholic' and 'Reformed'. This is because it emerged under Queen Elizabeth I's attempt to draw together those who wanted to preserve beliefs and practices from before the break with Rome (under Henry VIII) and those who wished to have more radical change. For this reason, the Anglican Church is a broad Church and spans a wide range of church styles. You may hear phrases such as 'high church' and 'low church'. These are attempts to describe whether a particular Church is drawn more towards the Reformed tradition (low church) or to the Catholic tradition (high church). Of course, within the range permitted by the Church of England there are many variations, such as liberal or charismatic. Most churches will fall in the midst of these various categories, and range from middle to high.

Indicators that an Anglican church is inclined towards the Catholic tradition

Such indicators may include the following:

- the Eucharist is celebrated daily and may even be called 'Mass';

- statues of Mary and the saints are in evidence and the lighting of votive candles may also be encouraged;

- the sacrament of the Eucharist is reserved;

- there are regular arrangements for confession;

- there are special priestly vestments for celebrating the Eucharist (for more information on this see *The Many Paths of Christianity,* page 39);

- incense and bells are used;

- the church may even have the service of Benediction (see under 'Monstrance' page 25).

Indicators that an Anglican church is inclined towards the Reformed or Evangelical tradition

Such indicators may include the following:

- the altar resembles a table;

- the Eucharist or Holy Communion is celebrated only a few times a month. The emphasis may be more on services such as Morning and Evening Prayer. This is becoming rare, as the Eucharist is growing in importance amongst Evangelicals;

- the vestments worn by the priest are less ornate;

- there are copies of the Bible in every pew.

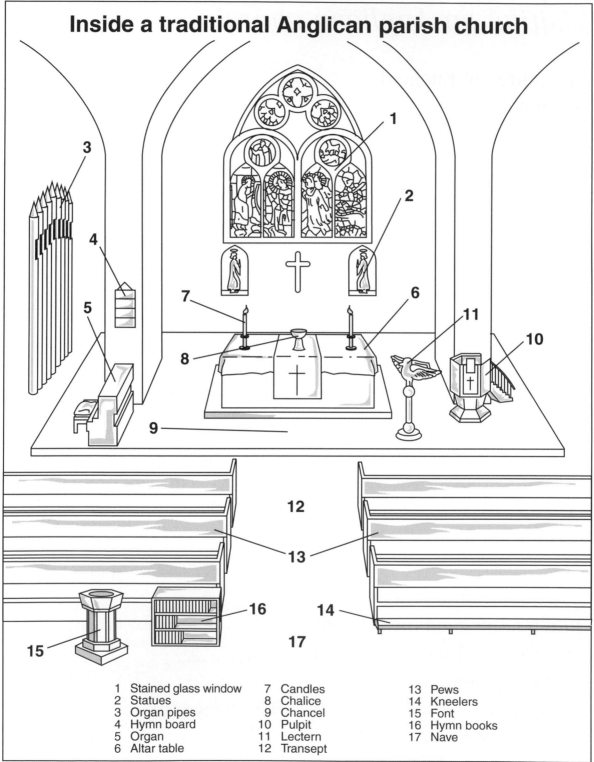

Inside a traditional Anglican parish church

1 Stained glass window	7 Candles	13 Pews
2 Statues	8 Chalice	14 Kneelers
3 Organ pipes	9 Chancel	15 Font
4 Hymn board	10 Pulpit	16 Hymn books
5 Organ	11 Lectern	17 Nave
6 Altar table	12 Transept	

Features of a typical Anglican parish church

In this section we will attempt to describe a fairly typical 'middle-of-the road' Anglican parish church. The plan on page 32 is fairly standard, but many modern churches are built in different shapes and sizes.

Figure 17

FONT (FIGURE 18)

Figure 18

Many Anglican churches still have a static stone or wooden font by the main west door. This symbolises that entry into the Christian family is through the waters of baptism. Many churches today do not use these fonts as they prefer to have baptisms during Sunday morning worship in full view of the congregation. On these occasions, a simple movable font or a bowl is used at the front of the church (Figure 19).

The old fonts can be very elaborate, with beautiful carved wooden covers which can be raised or lowered over the font like a lid. These may be covered with intricate Christian symbols.

BAPTISM (FIGURE 19)

In the Anglican Church, people of all ages may be baptised, but infant baptism is common, with

Figure 19

godparents making vows on behalf of the child. Anglican baptisms are similar to the baptismal rite of the Roman Catholic tradition (see page 28).

THE EASTER OR PASCHAL CANDLE

Often you will see a large candle by the font. This Easter or Paschal candle is first lit at the Easter vigil and subsequently on Sundays, major festivals and at baptisms (see also page 28).

THE ALTAR (FIGURE 20)

The most prominent feature in an Anglican church is the altar. It is traditionally placed at the east end of the church to signify the rising sun, which symbolises the resurrection of Jesus. Facing east is also facing Jerusalem, where Jesus died, and where Christians believe he rose and ascended into heaven.

The altar is where the Eucharist or Holy Communion is celebrated. This is one of the most important liturgies within the Anglican Communion world-wide. In this service, the Last Supper of Jesus is celebrated. If there is a perpetual light and tabernacle, this indicates the importance given to the Eucharist within the life of this community (see also pages 23–24).

Altars will often have a front cover which is coloured according to the particular season (see below). It may be decorated with Christian symbols such as those in Figure 21).

Many high altars have beautiful and ornate altarpieces, behind and above the altar. Some of these may be in the form of a triptych, as in Figure 22. They usually depict Jesus and the saints. They may also depict a scene from the life of Christ such as the Last

Figure 20

Supper or the Resurrection. If the altar-piece is a triptych, this will be closed during Lent to reinforce the need for a solemn preparation for Easter. It will then be re-opened for the Easter vigil and Easter day. Some churches not only close the triptych, but also cover all statues with purple cloth or sack cloth during Lent. The transformation of a church from Lent to Easter can be very dramatic, with a drab building suddenly being re-instated to its former glory, with a splash of colour and beautiful flower arrangements. This signifies the passing from death to life, not just for Jesus, but for the whole Christian community.

As in the Roman Catholic Church, most altars have been moved closer to the people to encourage more active participation of the laity within worship.

Figure 21

Figure 22

THE PULPIT (FIGURE 23)

The pulpit is usually on one side as you face towards the high altar. It is an elevated platform so that the congregation can both see and hear whoever is preaching the sermon. Pulpits in older churches can be elaborately carved in wood or stone. On the wall behind the pulpit there is usually a cross or crucifix as a reminder of the words of St Paul: 'I would think of nothing but Christ – Christ nailed to the cross' (1 Cor. 2: 2). There may be many different varieties of cross within the church. For an overview of some of these, with explanations of their significance, see pages 61–3 of *Religious Artefacts in the Classroom*.

Figure 24

represent the Good News being spread throughout the world, which in turn is represented by the globe that the eagle is perched upon. The eagle is an awe-inspiring bird and probably represents the majestic nature of the Word of God. It is also the symbol of St John the Evangelist.

THE ROOD SCREEN (FIGURE 25)

Some churches still have a screen separating the sanctuary from the main body of the church. This is a rood screen ('rood' means crucifix), and reminds

Figure 23

THE LECTERN (FIGURE 24)

The lectern is used for readings from the Bible. It may be a simple book stand or it may be beautiful and ornate. The classic 'eagle lectern' can be seen in the photograph. It is an intricate brass golden eagle with outstretched wings which hold the Bible. This is rich in symbolic meaning. The outstretched wings

Figure 25

us a little of the iconostasis within the Orthodox Church (see pages 45–46). Most of the original rood screens in pre-Reformation churches were destroyed or removed during the time of Cromwell.

SIDE CHAPELS

Many Anglican churches have more than one altar. Side chapels may be dedicated to a saint, or if it is a Lady Chapel, to the Virgin Mary. If there is a midweek Eucharist, it may take place at one of the side chapels where it is more appropriate for a smaller congregation.

KNEELER FOR CONFESSION (FIGURE 26)

Sometimes, by the side chapel you may see two chairs at right angles to each other. This is for individual confession to a priest (see also the Roman Catholic Church, pages 27–28).

Figure 26

FLAGS AND BANNERS (FIGURE 27)

Because the Anglican Church is the established church within England, there may be patriotic artefacts such as the national flag and memorials to the dead of the two Great Wars. Banners belonging to national organisations such as the Mothers' Union, Scouts and Guides and so on, can also be found.

STATUES

Not all Anglican churches will have statues, but if they do, they will usually be of the patron saint of that particular church, or of Mary, the mother of Jesus (Figure 28).

THE ORGAN

There is a great musical tradition within the Anglican Church as a whole. Many Anglican parishes, too, place great importance on music within worship. Organs in some churches are old and of great historical interest. Today, other instruments may be used in worship, such as guitar, drums, flutes, among others.

MEMORIALS

Most churches have individual or family memorials within the church building. These often

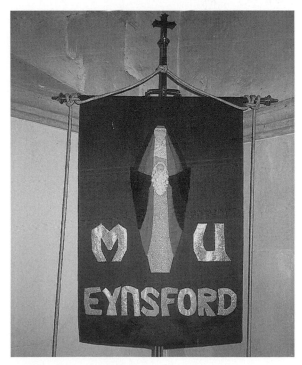

Figure 27

Figure 28

commemorate those who were popular within the community or who left a significant donation towards the upkeep or refurbishment of the church fabric. There may also be a memorial book for those who have died over the last decade. This can often be found in a glass case and is carefully updated and inscribed with beautiful calligraphy.

STAINED GLASS WINDOWS (FIGURE 29)

Anglican churches have a fine tradition of stained glass windows. These can be useful focal points within a school visit as they often refer to key moments in the life of Christ along with his parables and miracles. They may also contain a wealth of Christian symbols depicting, for example, the three Persons of the Trinity. Stained glass windows were designed to provide some form of religious education to a largely illiterate congregation!

Figure 29

LITURGICAL COLOURS

Different seasons within the Anglican liturgical year have their own symbolic colours. Most of these are shared with the Roman Catholic tradition.

These colours express the moods and significance of the different festivals. For example:

- **Green**: growth in faith
- **Red**: the blood of saints and martyrs; also the fire of the Holy Spirit at Pentecost
- **Purple**: a solemn colour representing the need for penitence and to make ready for a major festival, such as Lent, as preparation for Easter, and Advent, before Christmas.
- **White and/or gold**: joyful festivals such as Christmas and Easter day.

The above colours can be found on the altar front cover, the priest's vestments and adornments to the pulpit and lectern.

CHRISTMAS CRIB AND EASTER GARDEN (FIGURE 30)

Many churches have a focal point for Christmas and Easter. The photograph here shows a typical Nativity

Figure 30

scene. Christmas cribs depicting the birth of Jesus are very popular in Anglican churches. You may also see an Easter garden, which is made and displayed during the festival of Easter. This usually depicts both the scene of Golgotha (the Crucifixion) and the empty tomb, signifying the Resurrection of Jesus. Both these visual aids are particularly enjoyed by children.

KNEELERS (FIGURE 31)

Figure 31

Kneelers within a church can be a rich resource for any exploration of Christian symbols. These are often made by skilled individuals – mostly women – who take great pride in their handiwork.

PRAYER BOOKS

Some churches will provide complete prayer books for their congregation, but they are expensive and often members are encouraged to purchase their own for use at home for private meditation as well as for use in the church. Sometimes these will be paid for by a donation or legacy to the community. Generally, however, churches will provide specialised booklets which only contain the order of service for the Eucharist or for Morning and Evening Prayer, as these are less expensive and generally easier to follow.

Prayer books are a useful resource in the classroom as they contain material for exploring Christian (in this case Anglican) beliefs about marriage, death, initiation and so on.

HYMN BOOKS

Hymn books come in a variety of forms. Again they are a useful source for examining Christian beliefs – for example, about the mystery of the Trinity, the humanity and divinity of Jesus and so on. They can also be useful for exploring the nature and significance of Christian festivals, especially if they have a thematic index.

THE CHURCH HALL

As a parish church is also a centre for the local community, it usually has an attached hall which is used for a variety of activities. This may be used by many different groups who do not necessarily belong to the church as a worshipping community. It can be quite revealing for pupils to look at the diverse nature of the activities that take place there.

Possible activities for pupils

1 Sit quietly in the main body of the church and consider what you can hear, smell and see. How does this building make you feel? (See also pages 13–14).

2 Using the information on page 31, try to establish whether the church you are visiting is a high, middle, or low, Anglican church. Ask the priest his or her views on this. Which do you prefer? Explain why.

3 Draw or photograph some of the key features, such as the altar, font, pulpit or lectern, and research their function and significance in Christian worship.

4 Hunt the symbol! Draw or photograph some of the symbols found within the church and research their meaning. Design your own symbol to express your own feelings about this church.

5 Draw a chart showing the colours used during the liturgical year. What colours do you associate with different seasons of the year?

6 If the stained glass windows depict stories from the Bible, look these up and explore their significance for Christians.

7 Interview the priest about a day in her or his life. Seek their views on a variety of issues, such as:

– the ordination of women (pupils could explore their own views on this issue);

– whether the Church of England should remain established (i.e, should be the state Church);

– decision-making within the Church of England, locally, nationally and globally within the world-wide Anglican Communion.

8 Ask the priest to take the class through a

simulated baptism, exploring some of the symbols used.

9 Find out what kind of activities the church is involved in, and the service it aims to provide for the local community.

10 Look at hymns for different festivals and explore what they reveal about key Christian beliefs. Compose a tune to a Christian hymn, trying to capture its mood and ideas.

11 Role-play a scenario where a legacy of £30,000 has been left to the church. Pupils in the role of members of the Parochial Church Council must decide how to spend the money. Does it go to repair the church organ; repair the roof, which is badly leaking; or update the church hall so that it can be used as a day centre for the elderly?

Visiting an Orthodox church

Background

There are many different types of Orthodox Church within the United Kingdom which are linked with particular ethnic groups: Greek, Russian (Figure 32), Serbian, Coptic, Ethiopian, Syrian and so on. In this section we will focus mainly on the Greek Orthodox tradition, drawing upon differences between Orthodox Churches where appropriate. It is estimated that there are about half a million Orthodox Christians living in Britain today. Most of these come from the Greek Orthodox tradition, having come from Cyprus to Britain.

Figure 32

The Orthodox Church and the Roman Catholic Church split during the Great Schism of 1054. There were a variety of reasons why the One Church divided with such acrimony. For example, should the Pope in Rome have precedence over the Patriarch of Constantinople? Who was the real successor of St Peter? There was also a fundamental disagreement concerning the Trinity and particularly on the Holy Spirit as expressed within the formulation of creeds. The Western view, expressed in the Nicene Creed, states that the Holy Spirit 'proceeds from the Father and the Son', whereas in the Orthodox tradition the Holy Spirit proceeds from 'the Father'. Orthodox Christianity claims that the Western view subordinates the Holy Spirit to the Son and therefore diminishes the Holy Spirit as an equal and distinct Person within the Holy Trinity.

What you might see
ICONS (FIGURE 33)

The first thing you will notice on entering an Orthodox church is that the walls are often covered with icons.

'Icon' means literally 'image', and, according to tradition, the first icon was painted by Luke the Evangelist. His subject was of Mary holding the child Jesus. However, the oldest known icons go back to the fourth to the sixth centuries.

There are strict rules about how icons should be painted – not just the artistic style, but also the prayerful way in which they are created. Icons are not naturalistic but highly stylised and full of symbol.

Figure 33

Even the medium of the painting is significant. Icons use paint mixed with egg tempera, which not only enhances the colours used but also has a deep theological significance. The egg yolk used symbolises the earthiness of humankind's endeavours – an earthiness which is also part of God's creation and therefore blessed rather than despised.

Icons are not designed as illustrations of Biblical events or simply to be observed, as in Western art. They are created in order to draw the observer into the spiritual reality that the icon conveys. In fact an icon is not just a representation of the sacred, but is in itself sacred. When Orthodox Christians come face to face with an icon they will kiss it and light a candle before it. It is almost as if they are greeting a loved one, a member of their family.

For example:

cave	represents darkness and death
figures outside a cave	coming from darkness into Christ's light
mountains	often highly stylised, they remind us of Mount Sinai and closeness to God
inverse perspective	sometimes furniture will use an inverse perspective in order to invite the observer to step into the painting
rays from on high with 3 spikes	the Trinity
a tree	the Tree of Life

Figure 34

In an Orthodox church you will see icons of Jesus, Mary, angels and saints. Each one is stylised as shown below.

ICONS OF CHRIST

• *The Mandylion* (Figure 34) – this is based upon the tradition that Jesus' face was wiped by Veronica (literally 'true likeness') on his way to crucifixion. A miraculous image of the face of Christ was left on the veil and this has been the template for all Orthodox iconography ever since. There has been speculation that Veronica's cloth and the Shroud of Turin are one and the same.

• *Christ Pantocrator* (Figure 35) – this means Christ the Almighty, shown in majestic and solemn glory. In his left hand he holds a jewelled Bible which is either open or closed. His right hand is depicted in stylised blessing.

ICONS OF MARY

There are three main icons depicting Mary with the child Jesus. They are:

• *Virgin Orans* or *Virgin of the Sign* (Figure 36) – this shows Mary with her hands raised in a gesture of solemn prayer. The Christ child is placed in the centre within a large, round medallion upon Mary's breast.

• *Virgin Eleousa* or *Virgin of Vladimir* (Figure 37) – Eleousa means merciful or loving-kindness in Greek. In this representation, Mary's eyes are full of sadness as she foresees the passion and death of her son. There is a wonderful tenderness between mother and child as they embrace.

Figure 36

Figure 35

Figure 37

Figure 38

• *Virgin Hodigitria* (Figure 38) – this means 'the one who shows the way'. In this icon, Mary holds the child in her left arm and points to the babe with her right hand.

CANDLES (FIGURE 39)

On entering the church, the worshipper will give a donation of money, kiss an icon and light a candle, placing it in one of the many sand trays placed throughout the church. Prayers are said to the saints, who are believed to intercede on behalf of the faithful. The lighting of so many candles all around the church and the effect of the flickering flames on the metal elements of some of the icons can be very awe-inspiring. Children find it magical.

ICONOSTASIS (FIGURE 40)

The most striking feature of any Orthodox church is the huge, ornate screen which separates the altar from the main body of the church and the congregation. This screen is called an iconostasis and is usually covered with icons of Jesus, Mary, angels and the saints. It has three doors. The central door is known as the Royal door and the two on either side are called the North and South doors (Figure 41).

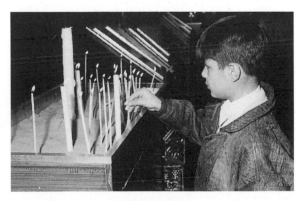

Figure 39

Figure 40

The iconostasis may remind you of the rood screen which is still found in some Anglican churches and cathedrals (see page 36). Only the priest may enter through the doors of the iconostasis. It reminds us a little of the 'Holy of Holies' of the ancient Jewish Temple of Jerusalem. It is behind this screen that the Eucharist or Divine Liturgy is celebrated.

The iconostasis represents the barrier between heaven and earth, between the sacred and the profane, between spiritual and material things. (Figure 41).

During the celebration of the Divine Liturgy, the priest will consecrate the bread and wine behind the closed doors of the iconostasis. He will then emerge through the central Royal door to give communion to the faithful. This emergence of the priest through the Royal door of the icon screen

shows how the gift of bread and wine is a gift from Paradise of Jesus' Body and Blood – a gift which in turn draws the faithful into the life of paradise (Figure 43).

Communion is given to each member of the congregation on a long-handled spoon. The consecrated bread is placed in a large chalice together with the consecrated wine, so that the two elements are given together.

For further information on the rich symbolism associated with the Divine Liturgy, see the section on the making of the communion bread or Prosphora on pages 18–19 of *Religious Artefacts in the Classroom.*

Often there are no seats or pews for the congregation, as they are used to standing for the entire service which may last for several hours.

Figure 41

BAPTISM (FIGURE 44)

This photograph shows the vast, ornate basin used for baptism. Infant baptism is encouraged within the Orthodox tradition. The child becomes a member of the Church through baptism. Oil, such as olive oil, is added to the water which has been warmed. The baby is completely undressed and then immersed three times in the water, in the name of the Father, the Son and the Holy Spirit. The child is given a name of a relation or saint and is then 'confirmed' with the Holy Spirit at the same ceremony. Holy oil, known as chrism, is used to make the sign of the cross on the baby's forehead. The act of

Figure 42

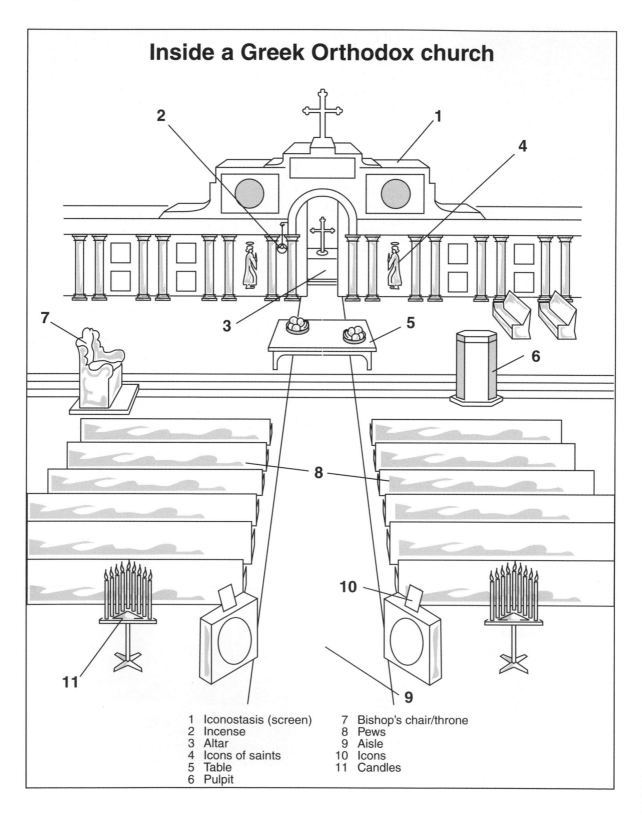

Inside a Greek Orthodox church

1	Iconostasis (screen)	7	Bishop's chair/throne
2	Incense	8	Pews
3	Altar	9	Aisle
4	Icons of saints	10	Icons
5	Table	11	Candles
6	Pulpit		

Figure 43

confirmation at an Orthodox baptism is different from the Roman Catholic and Anglican practice which is generally undertaken when candidates are in their mid-teens.

The Orthodox justification for this practice is as follows. The Christian faith is a mystery. Therefore it does not matter how old you are, it will always remain a mystery!

THE BIBLE

The Bible is often large and beautifully presented with ornate silver decorations in order to demonstrate its authority within the lives of the faithful.

CLASSROOMS

As an Orthodox church is very much a focal point for the community, there may be rooms attached for a variety of social functions. This might include classrooms for learning languages such as Greek.

Possible activities for pupils

I   Find photographs or reproductions of icons and explore some of the symbols and stylistic devices within them, and what they tell us about Orthodox beliefs and practices. Choose one and consider the following:

Figure 44

- do you like it?

- how does it make you feel?

- what would you like to ask the artist?

2   Interview an Orthodox Christian about:

- their favourite icons and the reasons for their choice;

- how being a Christian affects their daily life

3   Research into what happens at a Greek Orthodox wedding. Make a chart of the symbols used and what they represent.

4   Set up the classroom or a quiet area within the school as a darkened room. Light one or two candles and listen to a tape/CD of some Orthodox music. How does this music make you feel?

General introduction to Protestant churches

Background

Protestant Churches were new Churches which emerged on the Continent during the Reformation of the sixteenth century. They were called 'Protestant' because of their protest against the existing Church in the West, which was Roman Catholic. As this movement spread to England, the new Churches were independent of the established Church of England. They are also called Nonconformist Churches or Free Churches, because they refused to conform to the beliefs and practices of the established Churches.

The main Protestant denominations in England are the United Reformed Church (originally Presbyterians and Congregationalists), Baptists and Methodists.

Individual Protestant churches still prize their independence. Although they may belong to organisations like the Baptist Union, you will find a lot of autonomy in the individual churches. This often makes it difficult to generalise about Protestant Churches, and all the more important for pupils to be taken on visits to particular churches to find out about their ways of doing things.

Protestant church buildings tend to be plain. This was a reaction to the colourful imagery found in Roman Catholicism. Protestants have always emphasised the importance of inner belief rather than outward symbols. Often the only visual symbol will be a plain cross. The plain cross reminds Christians of Jesus' death and resurrection. They do not use crucifixes because they think this places all the emphasis on the death of Jesus rather than on the Resurrection. Some churches now use banners to proclaim their faith.

Figure 45

The seating in Protestant churches, whether pews or separate chairs, is purely practical. Modern churches may have movable furniture for flexibility. Balconies have no special significance: they were built to seat maximum numbers in the congregation. It is unlikely that you will see any kneelers, as Protestants usually sit or stand for prayer.

Music in Protestant churches is provided by whatever is in fashion. This used to be a piano or organ, and may be guitars and bands in modern churches. The singing of hymns is traditional and often choruses also, although some churches keep these for Sunday school. Modern churches tend to use modern Christian songs, in the tradition of choruses.

You will find some of your local Protestant churches listed in the Yellow Pages under 'Places of Worship'.

You may find entries such as 'Baptist church', but most will be listed under their place name, such as 'Orpington Methodist church' or 'New Cross Road Baptist church'. Some have religious names like 'Emmanuel Baptist church' or 'Living Flames Baptist church', and a few have saints' names like 'St Marks United Reformed and Methodist church'. The telephone number may be the minister's home number or the church office number.

Figure 47

Figure 46

Visiting a Baptist church

Background

The Baptist Church is one of the largest of the Protestant and Free Churches in the world. In 1996 it numbered 600,000 in the United Kingdom, with more than 2,000 churches. It is found throughout the world, particularly in Europe, where it began. Baptists settled in America from the mid-seventeenth century, and their missionary zeal in the nineteenth century led to a spectacular growth of the Baptist Church in the southern states: by 1950, there were 12 million Baptists in America, the largest number of Baptists world-wide.

A local Baptist church will have a minister, either a man or woman. He or she will have been trained at a Bible College and will have been chosen by the church's group of deacons, who meet regularly to decide on how the church is run. These decisions are influenced by the Church Meetings of its members.

Some Baptist Churches, particularly those known as Strict Baptist Churches, will only allow baptised Christians to be Church members. Others are much more open, allowing membership to any adult who 'believes in the Lord Jesus Christ for salvation'. Most Baptist Churches in the United Kingdom belong to the Baptist Union (formed in 1813) for mutual support, but they are not bound by it. Most also belong to the Baptist World Alliance (formed in 1905) to show that they are part of a world-wide Church. Many also belong to the British Council of Churches, showing their friendship towards Christians of other denominations.

History

Baptist Church buildings will be no more than 400 years old, and many are modern. The Baptist Church as we know it originated in 1609 when John Smyth and Thomas Helwys made the baptism of believers the basis of their Church in Amsterdam. At this time they baptised each other by pouring water over their heads. It was only later that they adopted the practice of full immersion.

Smyth and Helwys were Englishmen living as religious exiles in Holland. They were influenced by the Anabaptist movement of the Reformation, which itself goes back to earlier dissatisfaction with Church practices on baptism. Members of this Church returned to London in 1612. After the Restoration of the monarchy under Charles II in 1660, the Baptists formed one of the three main Protestant denominations in England.

Famous Baptists

The following are famous Baptists. You may well find reference to them in the Baptist churches you visit.

John Bunyan, author of The Pilgrim's Progress *(seventeenth century)*

William Carey, famous missionary (eighteenth century)

C. H. Spurgeon, preacher (nineteenth century) (Figure 48)

Martin Luther King, American civil rights leader (twentieth century)

Figure 48

What you might see
The Bible

When you enter a Baptist church, the focal point at the far end will be the place from which the Bible is read and the sermon preached. In older buildings this is usually a high platform built against the wall, with steps up to it. It will be particularly high in churches which have a balcony, so that the minister is between the congregations below and above him (Figure 49).

Sometimes the Bible is set out, open, on display. Or the Bible may be brought to the book stand and placed there as a sign that the service is about to start.

Figure 49

This focal point emphasises the importance for Baptists of the Bible, which they believe is the Word of God. Passages from the Bible will be read in their services. The minister will preach his sermon on the Bible readings, as well as referring to other passages from the Bible. Baptists will be encouraged to read the Bible daily, to learn short quotations from it (Bible tracts) and to find their way around it. Many Baptists take their own, well-thumbed Bibles to church with them, to follow the readings for themselves. You may also find some Bibles available at the back of the church or in the pews. Baptists believe that God speaks to people in their hearts when they think and pray about Bible passages, and they value each person's right to their own understanding of Scripture. For Baptists, as with other Protestants, the Bible has supreme authority in their lives.

BAPTISM

The Baptist Church got its name from its insistence on the importance of Believer's Baptism for salvation. Infants are not baptised in the Baptist Church, but only Christians who are old enough to make their own profession of faith. They are usually adults, but they may be teenagers or even younger if the minister and deacons are convinced of their belief. When someone is baptised, the minister may say: 'Do you confess Jesus Christ as your Lord and Saviour?' When the candidate says 'Yes', the minister will baptise him or her with words such as 'On the confession of your faith, I baptise you in the name of the Father, the Son and the Holy Spirit.'

Baptism in the Baptist Church is done by full immersion under water. We know that this is how the early Christians were baptised from Christian baptism pools that have survived from Roman times. Most Baptist churches will have their own baptistry or pool (Figure 50). Often this is covered by

Figure 50

floorboards, so that the space can be used during ordinary services, but some modern Baptist churches have the pool open and clearly visible. It is filled with warm water for a baptism, about waist high. The minister and candidate go down into the pool and the candidate is held securely and ducked right under the water. Some Baptists do this three times in the name of the Father, the Son and the Holy Spirit.

There used to be special clothes for baptism: white robes with weighted hems for the baptism candidates and waders for the minister. These days, most people wear ordinary, light-weight clothes that they can change out of easily after the service. Most Baptist ministers wear ordinary clothes, even for services.

COMMUNION

Communion is a very important service because it was given by Jesus himself at the Last Supper. To keep it special, Baptists usually take Communion only twice a month. But Baptists do not see anything 'magical' in it: they do not believe that the bread and wine change in any way. It is seen as an outward sign of personal faith and of communion or fellowship with each other. So it may be the custom for individuals to eat the piece of bread as soon as it is given to them, maybe with the words: 'This is the body of Christ broken for you. Feast on him by faith in your heart.' But they may wait for everyone to be served with their little glasses of wine (Figure 51) before they all drink together, when the minister may say, 'Let us drink to the praise and glory of Jesus.' There is no service book in the Baptist Church, so there are no set words. Ordinary bread is used and non-alcoholic wine/grape juice. (There is a teetotal tradition in the Baptist Church.)

The Communion service is conducted from a table, representing the meal-table around which Jesus

Figure 51

shared the Last Supper. Protestants do not call it an altar because they do not want to emphasise the idea of Jesus being sacrificed at the Communion service. The bread and wine are brought round to people as they stay in their seats.

Most Baptist churches give an open invitation for anyone who loves the Lord to share in Communion, but others, such as Strict Baptist Churches, may only share Communion with those who have received Believer's Baptism.

Possible activities for pupils

1 What surprised you most when you visited the Baptist church?

2 (a) Interview a recently baptised Baptist to find out what baptism meant to that person and how they felt during the ceremony.

   (b) Have you ever done something as an individual in a public ceremony? How did you feel?

3 Make a shoe-box model of a Baptist church, paying particular attention to the distinctive features.

4   Interview some Baptists about the importance of the Bible in their lives. Are there any books which have influenced your beliefs or way of life?

5   Find out about a famous Baptist, such as Charles Spurgeon.

6   Are there banners in the church you have visited? What Christian teachings do they proclaim? Make a paper banner proclaiming something that you think is important.

7   Compare a Baptist church with that of another Christian denomination, such as a Roman Catholic church. What do the similarities and differences tell us about the main beliefs of these two Christian traditions?

8   Interview Baptists about why they do not use images or many symbols within their place of worship.

Visiting a Methodist church

Background

The Methodist Church broke away from the Church of England in the eighteenth century. It was founded by John Wesley (1703–91). John was a Church of England priest who was influenced by Protestant beliefs such as the importance of personal conversion in order to be saved. He himself had such an experience on 24 May 1738, after being a priest for ten years, and described it in this way:

> **I felt my heart strangely warmed. I felt I did trust in Christ, Christ alone for salvation and an assurance was given me that he had taken away my sins, even mine**.

When churches closed their doors to him, he began preaching in the open air (Figure 52) and attracted huge crowds. He organised his followers into small groups for prayer meetings, but still encouraged them to attend their parish church services. However, as time went by, the movement grew with its own carefully organised structure and ordained ministers. When, in 1784, John Wesley appointed a conference of a hundred men to continue the Methodist movement after his death, it was clear that this was now a Church in its own right.

The name 'Methodist' was originally a nickname from the time when John was a fellow at Oxford. There he gathered round him a group of Christians who held weekly meetings for Bible study and prayer, and were known for their earnest and methodical approach. John's brother, Charles, belonged to this group and was one of the leaders of the Methodist movement, although remaining within the Church of England. He is remembered particularly for his hymn-writing. He wrote more than 5,500 hymns, many of which are well known, such as 'Hark, the herald angels sing'.

Figure 52

John Wesley travelled widely on his preaching missions, covering about 8,000 miles a year on horseback and 250,000 miles by the time he died. He wrote thousands of letters and preached more than 40,000 sermons. When he died, there were more than 70,000 Methodists in Britain and 294 preachers. Methodism had also spread to America and the West Indies. 'The world is my parish' is one of John Wesley's best-known sayings. Today there are 54 million Methodists, in every continent of the world. The largest Methodist Church population is in the United States. There are about 1,300,000 Methodists in the United Kingdom today.

Church buildings

Some Methodist Church buildings are from the nineteenth century. Others, like the one below, are modern (Figure 53). An important feature of a Methodist church building is that it is more than a place of worship: there are a number of rooms for other clubs and activities.

Figure 53

Look out for leaflets which give information about the life and work of the church. You should see notice-boards outside (Figure 54) giving times of services, and there may be posters like the one here at Christmas time which says: 'Jesus the best gift. Come in and join us.' (Figure 53)

THE BRENT METHODIST CHURCH

Sunday Celebrations 10.45am & 6.30pm
Sunday School   10.45am

We are here to care in the name of Jesus.
If you need help or further information
about our other services and weekday
activities please contact:-

The Minister - Rev. Nigel Barton, 01322 220514 or
Layworkers - Marilyn & Micheal Manning, 01322 273506

Figure 54

Figure 55

Church organisation and leadership

The Methodist Church has ordained ministers, both men and women. They are given the title 'Reverend'. They usually have pastoral responsibility for a particular church, but are also part of a local 'circuit' of churches and will take services at times in all of these (Figure 55).

Many people take part in organising and leading services as well as the minister. They are called 'lay' people, meaning that they are not ordained. There are local preachers attached to each circuit who will be on a rota for preaching in the different churches. There are lay assistants at the individual churches who make sure that everything is ready for the service. Other people may do the Bible readings or say prayers; a small group of singers and musicians may lead from the front – some may take part in drama or dance, some may be asked to do a short talk as part of the sermon.

Membership

Membership in the Methodist Church is regarded as an adult commitment, although children are welcome at church and may attend Junior Church/Sunday School, or come to clubs that it runs. The Methodist

Association of Youth Clubs is one of the largest organisations in Europe.

Membership takes place at the same time as confirmation and candidates must be teenagers or older. The candidates come to the front of the church and kneel down before the minister who lays his or her hands on their heads to confirm them, and may then shake them by the right hand to welcome them into full membership. They are given a membership card which is renewed annually. They renew their commitment to Christ each year at the Covenant Service, which usually takes place on the first Sunday in January. A covenant is a two-way agreement between God and his people and is a very important Biblical idea. At this service, Methodists offer their lives and all that they have to be used in God's service. In return, they believe that God accepts them as they are and will help them in the coming year to be what he wants them to be.

What you might see
LOGO (FIGURE 56)

Figure 56

CROSS (FIGURE 57)

As with other Protestant Churches, a plain cross is used, to show the importance of Jesus' Resurrection. It is often a focal point in the church.

Figure 57

PULPIT (FIGURE 58)

The pulpit is the key feature of a Methodist Church building and is often very large and imposing. It was originally built at the front of the church, in the centre, but is now placed to one side. When we remember how John Wesley spread the Good News of Christianity through his sermons, it is not surprising to find that the sermon is the main part of a Methodist service. The sermon encourages Methodists to apply the Bible to their everyday lives. Methodism has always been involved with social issues, particularly among the working classes. The Home Mission Division says:

> **Whether we are caring for ex-prisoners, organising a petition, raising money for famine relief, or writing to our members of Parliament, we are acting in response to Jesus who said 'love one another as I have loved you.'**

Figure 58

Figure 59

THE BIBLE (FIGURE 59)

A large Bible is read from the pulpit of the Brent Methodist church and another is set out symbolically on the Holy Communion table in the centre at the front of the church. Look out for Bibles in the church you visit. The Methodist Church was founded on Bible study and seeing the relevance of this for today.

MUSIC

Music is very important in Methodist Church services. This Church was born in song, with Charles Wesley's hymns, many of which are in the Methodist Hymn Book, called *Hymns and Psalms*. They may use other hymn books as well, for modern Christian songs. Methodists still find that God speaks to them through the hymns and that they can express and strengthen their faith by singing them. The congregation stands to sing hymns between the talks, Bible readings and prayers.

Many older buildings have large, elaborate pipe organs, to play music before and after the service

Figure 60

and to accompany the hymns. They may also have modern musical instruments, such as keyboards, guitars and drums.

THE COMMUNION TABLE (FIGURE 60)

When Methodism started there were not enough ministers to celebrate Holy Communion regularly in every church, and ministers travelled from one to the other. So Methodism could not celebrate Holy Communion, or 'the Lord's Supper', as frequently as the Anglicans. Today there are usually two

Figure 61

celebrations a month, one at a morning service and one in the evening.

The altar or Communion table is therefore less significant in Methodist churches and is usually a simple but attractive wooden table at the front of the church. When not in use, it will probably have a vase of flowers on it and the Bible may be out on display there. When in use it is covered with a white cloth, and the bread and wine is put there before the service and covered over. The cloth in the photograph has 'IHS' on it, which are the first three letters of the Greek word for 'Jesus'. They may be embroidered with other relevant symbols, or words such as 'I am the Bread of Life'. The wooden Communion table in the photograph (Figure 59) has the words of Jesus carved on it: 'This do in remembrance of me.'

The Holy Communion service is very important because it commemorates the Last Supper that Jesus ate with his disciples, when he left them bread and wine to remember him by. A Methodist leaflet explains that this is a means of receiving Jesus' Spirit into their lives: 'In this way all that is wrong in our lives can be dealt with and we are given hope and strength for the future' ('The Methodist Church: Our

Figure 62

Motivation, Our Message, Our Mission, For over 250 Years' published by the Home Mission Division). The service for Holy Communion is found with other Methodist services in *The Methodist Service Book*, which owes much to the Anglican Book of Common Prayer. A booklet containing just the section on Holy Communion gives these general directions:

> **It is the privilege and duty of members of the Methodist Church to avail themselves of this Sacrament. Communicant members of other Churches whose discipline so permits are also welcome to receive it.**
> **('The Sunday Service', published by the Methodist Conference Office, 1974).**

A Methodist minister takes this service. People come and kneel at the Communion rail to receive first a piece of bread and then a small glass of grape juice (since Methodists do not allow alcohol on their

church premises). There are holes in the Communion rail for the empty glasses (Figures 61 and 62).

THE FONT (FIGURE 63)

Infant baptism or dedication is practised in the Methodist Church, but the font is not given any great prominence. Here it is used as a flower stand when not in use for baptisms, and in some churches a simple bowl may be brought out for the purpose.

The cradle roll, with the names of children who have been baptised, is displayed in church. Parents are also given baptism certificates to keep.

BANNERS (FIGURE 64)

Look out for banners which proclaim the Christian faith. This one has been put up specially for Christmas time. Emmanuel means 'God with us' and

Figure 63

Figure 64

is the name for Jesus used in the Christmas story of Matthew's Gospel.

BOOKSTALL

Many churches have bookstalls, to encourage their members to read devotional books so as to help them lead Christian lives.

Possible activities for pupils

1 (a) Find out more about the life of John Wesley, concentrating on the most important events of his life.

    (b) What influenced John's religious views (including family background and childhood experiences)?

    (c) What has influenced your own religious beliefs and practices or lack of them?

2 (a) Can you remember what it felt like to go to a new school for the first time? What can be done to make newcomers feel welcome?

    (b) Find out how Methodists try to make newcomers welcome at their services.

    (c) Design your own poster to encourage people to come to church.

3 (a) List the range of activities which go on throughout the week at the Methodist church you visit.

    (b) Find out more about one of these.

4 Interview a Methodist minister to find out about his or her ordination and ministry. In groups, prepare some questions beforehand.

5 (a) Are you a member of any organisation, and what did you do to become a member?

    (b) Ask some Methodists what membership of their Church means for them.

6   If you had the opportunity to preach to a large congregation of people, what would you want to say? Think about something which you feel strongly about, and prepare a short speech about it. (One or two of these speeches could be delivered from the pulpit when you visit a Methodist church, or from a soap-box back in school. They could be used in collective worship.)

7   (a)   What type of music do you like and how important is it in your life?

    (b)   Find and list the first lines of some of Charles Wesley's hymns.

    (c)   Copy out some lines or verses of your choice and say what you think they mean.

    (d)   Make up a poem of your own that could be used as a religious song.

8   Working in groups, make a large paper or cloth banner which would be suitable for a Methodist church. Display them in the RE room.

9   Look at the range of books displayed on the bookstall. List at least two titles, and explain how they would help someone in their Christian lives.

Visiting a United Reformed church

Background

The United Reformed Church, as its name suggests, was formed from the union of a number of existing Churches. It was the first union of its kind since the Reformation, when the Churches split up. Three Churches have joined together in the United Reformed Church. The first two united in 1972. They were the Congregational Church in England and Wales and the Presbyterian Church in England. Later, in 1981, the Reformed Association of the Churches of Christ also joined, a Church which had begun in the United States among Christians who had come from Scotland. This enabled it to be called the United Reformed Church in the United Kingdom because it now had members from England, Wales and Scotland.

Figure 65

Figure 66

Ecumenism (Figure 66)

This noun comes from a Greek word for the whole inhabited world, and has come to be used by a modern movement in the Church which seeks world-wide Christian unity. The ecumenical movement of the twentieth century has had an effect among many Churches locally, nationally and internationally. For instance, local Churches of different denominations may hold joint services or share a building.

There are a number of national organisations which bring Churches together such as the Council of Churches for Britain and Ireland and the Free Church Federal Council. At the international level there are organisations such as the World Council of Churches and Christian Aid. The photograph shows

the emblem of the World Council of Churches: the ship of faith, with a cross for its mast, tossed on the waters of the world. This symbol was embroidered on to the cloth hanging from the pulpit in a United Reformed church.

At the original service of union in Westminster Abbey for the United Reformed Church, the following declaration was read out, explaining why they believed it was important for Christians to join together.

> **The United Reformed Church declares its intention in fellowship with all the Churches, to pray and work for such visible unity of the whole Church as Christ wills … in order that men and nations may be led more and more to glorify the Father in heaven.**

The URC is committed to further unity with other Churches and continues to work with other Christians wherever possible. Most of these partnerships are with Methodist and Anglican Churches.

What you might see
THE CELTIC CROSS (FIGURE 67)

The first symbol of the United Reformed Church was a Celtic cross. The cross is important as the central symbol of Christianity, and the Celtic style reflects the Scottish origins of the Churches which united. The Presbyterian Church started in Scotland under the leadership of John Knox (who had been influenced by the Continental reformer John Calvin).

Their current logo was adopted by the URC in 1981. It shows the plain cross and a fish. Remember that Protestants don't use a crucifix with the figure of Christ on it, but a plain cross to remind them of the Resurrection. The fish symbol was used by the early Christians and has been found on the walls of the catacombs in Rome. These were underground burial

Figure 67

Figure 68

chambers where the early Christians met for safety at times of persecution. The Greek word for 'fish' is ICHTHUS, and this symbol is a coded message based

on five Greek letters:

I – IESOUS – Jesus

CH- CHRISTOS – Christ

TH – THEOU – God's

U – HUIOS – Son

S – SOTER – Saviour

The fish was adopted by FURY (the Fellowship of United Reformed Youth) in 1972 as their badge.

Focal points

The positioning of certain features in the place of worship shows their importance for that particular church. Look out, therefore, to see which of the following are given the most prominent positions.

THE BIBLE (FIGURE 69)

For Protestants, the Bible is at the centre of their religion. It has the place of honour on the table at the front of a United Reformed church. When a service is about to begin, the congregation stands and the Bible is carried in and placed on the lectern, from where it will be read during the service. It is significant that the Bible enters first, before the minister. Many churches have Bibles in the pews so that people can follow the readings for themselves.

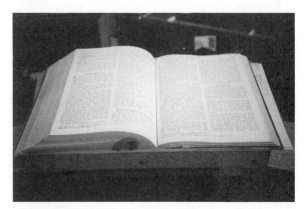

Figure 69

Figure 70

THE PULPIT (FIGURE 70)

Because the Bible is so important, the minister's sermon is also very important, when he or she will explain the Bible readings. Some churches have a pulpit for the sermon and a separate lectern for the readings; others will use either a pulpit or a lectern for both.

THE COMMUNION TABLE (FIGURE 71)

Communion is very important because it was established by Jesus himself at the Last Supper. The Communion table therefore has a prominent position in the church. Bread and wine are used because Jesus gave his followers bread to represent his body and wine to represent his blood. He told them to do this in remembrance of him. The bread and wine are known as 'the elements' in the URC. Other names may be used for Communion, such as 'the Communion of the Lord's Supper' and 'the Sacrament of Holy Communion'. Members of the Church are expected to attend Communion once a month, and it is provided at the morning service on

Figure 71

the first Sunday of the month and at the evening service on the third Sunday.

The minister and a few elders sit behind the table, facing the congregation. The table is laid with a cloth for Communion, as in the photograph. A large chalice (goblet) of wine and beautiful silver plates for the bread are placed on it. In some churches, people drink from individual glasses instead of the chalice. The photograph shows these special trays of glasses. The elders take the bread first to the people. If it is in small pieces, each person takes one. If it is a loaf of bread, each person pulls off a small piece and passes the loaf to the person next to them. Then the elders serve the wine. If it is in a chalice, people take a sip and pass it on. If it is in small glasses, they take one each from the tray. In some churches people wait for everyone to be served before eating or drinking, in others they eat and drink as soon as they are served.

THE FONT (FIGURE 72)

Baptism is also important because Jesus was baptised and he directed his followers to baptise people (Matthew 28: 19). It is the main sign of being a Christian and joining the world-wide Church. Parents may bring their baby to be baptised, or adults can be baptised and make the promises for themselves. They have to say that they believe in Jesus Christ and promise to follow him; that they believe and trust in

God and the Holy Spirit. They promise to worship God, to be a friend of Jesus and a friend of other Christians. Baptism usually takes place during the normal Sunday service, and the members of the Church promise to help the person 'live a Christian life in the family of God'.

A font may be used for baptism. This is a basin to hold the water for baptism and, as here, it is often a beautiful piece of furniture. The one shown here has its lid on. Baptism can be performed in different ways in the United Reformed Church. Sometimes the water is used to make the sign of the cross on the person's head and sometimes the water is poured over their head. Some United Reformed churches practise baptism by immersion in a baptistry (a special baptism pool), or even a lake or a river. The water is a sign of inner cleansing or

Figure 72

forgiveness. When the minister performs the baptism, he or she says, 'I baptise you in the name of the Father, the Son and the Holy Spirit.'

There is also a service of thanksgiving for the birth of a child. This is used by members of the Church who do not want to have their baby baptised but want their child to come to baptism at a later stage.

In the URC, a baptised person can decide to become a member of the Church. This is done at a Confirmation service or Profession of Faith. It can be done by the 'laying on of hands', when the person kneels before the minister, who places his hands on the person's head. Or the person is welcomed as a member of the Church by being offered 'the right hand of fellowship' (namely a hand-shake). The person repeats the promises made at his baptism, agrees to attend church regularly and to support the church and its work. In Protestant Churches, the ministers and the church expenses are paid for by the congregation. So becoming a member of the United Reformed Church is a serious commitment.

OFFERINGS (FIGURES 73 AND 74)

A collection of money is taken during the service. Cloth bags with wooden handles are passed round for people to put their money in. They are then piled on to the large metal plate and brought up to the front of the church where a prayer is said by the minister, offering the money to God for his work.

Figure 73

Figure 74

Many Church members will belong to a 'covenant' scheme where they promise to give a certain amount of money regularly. They are given little envelopes to put their money in. These are dated so that they remember to give what they promised. Churches rely on this regular giving to work out their budgets. Protestant Churches usually teach their members to give a tithe (that is, a tenth) of their earnings.

MUSIC (FIGURE 75)

Most churches will have some sort of keyboard instrument to accompany the hymn-singing. Traditionally, this was an organ or piano, but many now have electric keyboards. There is a United Reformed Church hymn book called *Rejoice and Sing*; and other hymnbooks may be used as well. There is a strong tradition of congregational singing. Some churches have a robed choir and special choir-pews; others may have a choir on an occasional basis.

Other features
SEATING

The seating is functional. There may be chairs or pews. The congregation remains seated for most of the service, including prayers.

Kneelers are only used when people come out to

Figure 75

the front of the church for special services such as weddings, reception into membership and healing by the laying-on of hands with prayer.

OTHER ROOMS

United Reformed churches usually have a number of different rooms as well as the main place of worship. These are used for social gatherings after the service and at other times during the week. They are often used by non-church groups such as nurseries. One of the rooms is called a vestry and it is where the ministers put on their special robes for the service.

Possible activities for pupils

1 Look up in a Bible/New Testament the following reference about Christian unity: (1 Corinthians 12: 12–31). What image is used of the Church? Try to illustrate what St Paul is saying.

2 Find out if the United Reformed church you have visited does anything with other local Christian denominations. What are the advantages and disadvantages of this?

3 Find out what this church calls the Communion service.

4 When you visit the church, ask if you can be shown round other rooms as well as the place of worship.

5 Pupils could make a list of what else goes on in the church building you visit. (This information is often found in Church magazines or leaflets.)

6 Discuss with other pupils and the person showing you around the church why the United Reformed Church likes its building to be used by local people, even if they are not church-goers. Do you think this is a good thing?

Visiting a Jewish synagogue

Introduction

The synagogue is an extension of the Jewish home. It is not a place for silence and reflection, but a busy and vibrant focal point for the Jewish community to meet and share worship, learning and life together.

HISTORY

Originally, the centre for Jewish worship was the Temple in Jerusalem. Here the priests, led by the High Priest, offered sacrifices to God on behalf of the people. It is likely that the local places of worship, called synagogues, started when the Jews were exiled in Babylon in the sixth century BCE. They became popular during the second century BCE even though the Jews had by this time returned to the Holy Land and rebuilt the Temple. The synagogues became the centres for the Pharisees, a movement of very devout, law-abiding Jews. The synagogues were 'meeting places' (the word means 'meeting' or 'assembly'), where ordinary people could gather to worship God through study of the Torah and for prayer. They were not just for worship, but also for religious education and social gatherings. This is still the case today.

There are two main types of Judaism: Orthodox and Progressive (for example, Reform and Liberal Judaism). Most synagogues in the United Kingdom are Orthodox, keeping all the traditional beliefs and practices of old, and conducting their services in Hebrew. Progressive Judaism believes that only the moral commandments in their Scriptures are binding on them, and that ritual laws may need to be adapted to modern times or abandoned altogether. Their services are in both Hebrew and the vernacular.

Most of the features which you will see are the same in Orthodox and Progressive synagogues. The main differences are that men and women sit apart in Orthodox synagogues and only the men lead the worship. In Reform and Liberal synagogues, men and women may sit together and the women can take a full part in public worship. Indeed, there are a number of women rabbis in the United Kingdom. The other main difference is in the layout of the synagogue. An Orthodox synagogue has a large reading platform (the *bimah*) in the centre, with the seating arranged on three sides of it and the Holy Ark on the fourth side. The Torah scroll is read

Figure 76

facing the Ark. A Progressive synagogue has the seating facing the front where the Holy Ark is placed. The Torah scroll is read facing the congregation. In an Orthodox synagogue, the Ark is always in the wall facing Jerusalem, but this is not always the case in Progressive synagogues.

What you might see
OUTSIDE THE SYNAGOGUE (FIGURE 76)

It is sometimes difficult to identify a synagogue from outside, since the need for security has led to a measure of secrecy. You may notice a Jewish symbol, such as the six-pointed Magen David ('shield of David'), known as the Star of David. Most modern, purpose-built synagogues now prefer to use the two tablets representing the Commandments as their symbol, rather than the Magen David.

'Mezuzah' means 'door-post', and is the name of a miniature scroll which is put in a case and fixed to the door-frame of Jewish buildings and rooms (Figure 77). The scroll is made from parchment and is hand-written in Hebrew (although printed copies can be obtained for use in school). The scroll contains the first two paragraphs of the Shema (Hebrew for 'Hear!'). The opening of the Shema in Deuteronomy 6: 4–5 sums up the essence of Judaism in these words:

Hear, O Israel:

The Lord our God, the Lord is One,

Love the Lord your God

with all your heart, and with all your soul,

and with all your strength.

The Shema goes on to say, 'Write them on the door-frames of your houses and on your gates' (verse 9), which is the origin of this custom. Jews touch the mezuzah case as they enter the building or room, and then kiss their fingers. It reminds them of the presence of the Almighty and that this building is run according to Jewish law. This placing of the mezuzah case on the synagogue door-post reinforces the point already made, that the synagogue is an extension of the Jewish home.

Figure 78

Figure 77

Key features inside the synagogue

MAIN FOYER: NOTICE-BOARDS

When you enter the foyer of a synagogue, take time to look at the range of activities advertised on the notice-boards. This gives pupils a real idea of some of the issues and concerns facing the Jewish community today. It reveals the synagogue as a meeting place and not just a place of worship. For example, an important element within Judaism is *Tzedekah* which is charity given for the upkeep of the synagogue and for the needy.

ARON HAKODESH – THE HOLY ARK (FIGURE 79)

Figure 80

Figure 79

Inside the synagogue, the most important part is the Holy Ark. This is where the Torah scrolls are kept. It may be a simple wooden cupboard or a structural part of the building. In the United Kingdom it is situated on the wall facing east, towards Jerusalem where the Temple once stood. The congregation face the *Aron Hakodesh* during worship. For most of the time the Holy Ark is covered with a beautiful curtain, usually of rich velvet. This may have Jewish symbols embroidered on it, such as the seven-branched candlestick or Menorah which once stood in the Temple, the crown and lions of Judah (one of the Jewish kingdoms) or the two tablets of the Ten Sayings (the Ten Commandments). Often the scrolls in the Ark are protected by a metal grill (Figure 80), as they are very valuable. (Note: The person showing you round will need to be asked beforehand to bring the key along if you want to see the Torah undressed.)

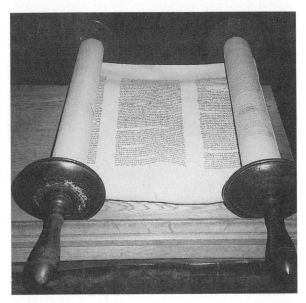

Figure 81

The Holy Ark gets its name from the Ark of the Covenant in the Bible. This was a special chest in which the Ten Commandments were kept (Exodus 25:10–22). This was portable in the time of Moses (Numbers 10: 33), but was eventually given a permanent place in the Temple in Jerusalem in the innermost part known as the Holy of Holies, behind the curtain of the temple. The Holy Ark in a synagogue now takes its place.

SEFER TORAH – TORAH SCROLL (FIGURES 81 AND 82)

When arranging your visit to a synagogue, ask if a Torah can be brought out of the Ark and unrolled a little for you to see. It is worth looking closely at the cover and decorations as well as the scroll itself, which is in Hebrew, hand-written on parchment. You will also notice how heavy it is, when it is lifted out of the Ark.

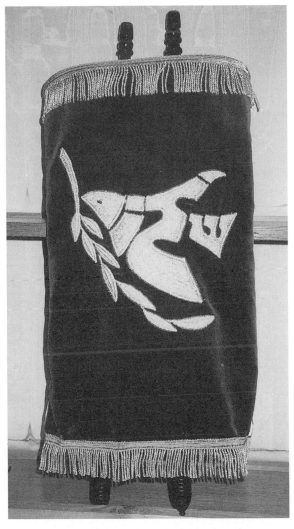

Figure 82

Each scroll contains the first five books of the Bible, known as the books of Moses. Jews believe that these are the laws God has given them to live by. They are hand-written on parchment which is rolled on to two wooden handles to form a scroll. Each synagogue will have at least two scrolls, so that when they come to the final reading they can continue immediately with the first part of the Torah. This happens at the annual celebration of Simchat Torah ('Rejoicing in the Law') and shows their eagerness to study the Torah.

A Torah has special coverings and ornaments which show its regal qualities as well as protecting it. They resemble the vestments worn by the high priest in ancient times. The priestly role was to bring people closer to God, and this is what the Torah now does.

Figure 83

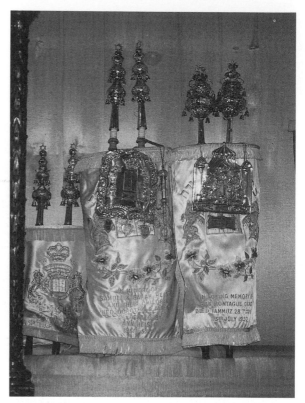

Figure 84

When the scroll is closed up, it is fastened with a Torah band and covered with a mantle, usually in rich, royal colours like red or blue, to show its importance. The mantles are often beautifully embroidered with Jewish symbols and sometimes have a dedication on them, if they were donated to a synagogue in memory of a loved one. Apart from the cloth mantle, scrolls may also be decorated with what looks like a metal shield, again with Jewish symbols on it (Figure 83). This is like the breastplate worn by the high priest two thousand years ago. Each pole is decorated with a crown, like the head-

dress of the high priest, and silver bells. The bells make a pleasant tinkling sound as the scroll is processed around the synagogue, so that people can hear it coming and treat it with respect.

A special white Torah cover is used for the high holy days of Yom Kippur (the Day of Atonement) and Rosh Hashanah (New Year). In this photograph you can also see a small scroll which is permanently kept in a white cover in memory of the victims of the Holocaust (Figure 84).

Most Torah scrolls that you are likely to see are of the Western European variety, as described above. The Jews who emigrated further south, into Spain, called Sephardi Jews, protect their scrolls in metal cases, like the one shown here (Figure 85). The catches can be released to open the scroll for reading. The scroll is turned using the handle on the top.

Figure 85

Figure 86

the Holy Ark (Figure 86). They are indicated by the shape of the two tablets on which Moses is said to have brought them down from Mount Sinai. On each tablet are the first two words of five of these laws. Notice the Hebrew word ('lo') for 'Not' ('Thou shalt not …').

NER TAMID – THE ETERNAL LIGHT

A perpetual light burns above the Holy Ark. This recalls the oil lamp that burned continually in the Temple above the most sacred part, the Holy of Holies, where the Ark of the Covenant was kept. It shows that God's laws in the Torah are sent to guide them. The light was traditionally an oil lamp, but is often lit by electricity today.

THE TEN SAYINGS (THE TEN COMMANDMENTS)

The Ten Sayings sum up all the laws of the Torah. They are so important that they are written up above

BIMAH (FIGURE 87)

This is the raised platform in the centre of Orthodox synagogues used mainly for the reading of the Torah and for the giving of the sermon. During the service, the Torah is carried in procession from the Ark to the *Bimah*, and then returned after it has been read.

SEATING (FIGURE 88)

Men and women are separated in Orthodox synagogues, just as they were in the Temple where they had separate courtyards. Since only men are allowed to lead worship in Orthodox synagogues, the women and children were traditionally accommodated in balconies. Modern synagogues may not have balconies but would still designate separate seating for women. The photograph shows a screen for them to sit behind.

Figure 87

Figure 88

Figure 89

SIDDUR – PRAYER BOOK (FIGURE 89)

'*Siddur*' means 'order' and is the name given to the Jewish prayer books because they give the *order* of service – that is, all the set prayers of the various services. These prayers are in Hebrew, but the vernacular is also given.

PRAYER FOR THE ROYAL FAMILY

The only prayer in a Jewish service which is not in Hebrew is the prayer for the rulers of the country where the synagogue is. This prayer is said in the language of that country. Throughout their history the Jews have been forced from their homeland to

settle in different parts of the world. Although Jews still think of Israel as their spiritual homeland, many are happily settled in other countries and want to show their loyalty to the host government.

TALLIT – PRAYER SHAWL (FIGURE 90)

The *tallit* is a prayer shawl traditionally worn by adult Jewish men. However, both young boys and women rabbis may be seen wearing prayer shawls in Reform and Liberal synagogues. It is worn over the shoulders or over the head when they pray, expressing the belief that God envelops them. It comes in various

Figure 90

Figure 91

sizes and designs, although traditionally they are large and white in colour with blue or black lines across each end. The most important features are the fringes on each end with long, knotted tassels in each corner which are called *tzitzit*. Numbers 15: 37–41 explains that these tassels are a reminder to them of the commandments (*mitzvah*).

KIPPAH/CAPUL/YAMULKA

Jews must cover their head when they pray to show respect to God above them. Some Jews wear a skull-cap, called a *kippah*, most of the time; others put it on for prayers. They are usually only worn by men but, once again, you may see woman rabbis wearing them in Reform and Liberal synagogues. Adult men and women should cover their heads during worship.
NB: *Teachers may be asked to cover their heads when visiting a synagogue, though this is not always insisted upon if you are not there to take part in worship. Sometimes, skull-caps are provided for male visitors.*

TEFILLIN – PHYLACTERIES (FIGURE 91)

The word 'phylactery' comes from the Greek for 'box', and '*tefillin*' is Hebrew for 'prayers'. They are two prayer-boxes which Jewish men tie to their upper arm and forehead during weekday prayer. The box and straps are made from leather and are painted black. Before the prayer-boxes are sealed, small parchment scrolls are inserted containing the same portions of the Shema as in the mezuzah as well as passages from Exodus 13. They are worn in fulfilment of the command 'Tie them as symbols on your hands and bind them on your foreheads' (Deuteronomy 6: 8). By having them on their heads and close to their hearts, they are showing that their hearts and minds are dedicated to God when they pray.

You may find some of them in the synagogue you visit, especially if the seating is allocated to particular individuals and has a space for storage.

HOLOCAUST MEMORIAL (FIGURE 92)

All synagogues in the United Kingdom will have a memorial to the six million Jews who perished during the Nazi Holocaust (the Shoah). Some of the Torah scrolls may also originate from synagogues plundered or destroyed by the Nazis.

Figure 92

Figure 93

SUKKAH (FIGURE 93)

Note: The first part of the Autumn term is not a good time to visit synagogues as there are many festivals which take place at this season and the Jewish community is very busy. However, if you do visit at a festival time, you may see things of interest related to the festival.

Sukkah means 'hut' and is the name of the temporary dwelling used during the festival of *Sukkot* (Tabernacles). This is an autumn harvest festival, and during the week of *Sukkot* Jews gather together in their huts to share food and thank God for his goodness. Jews make them in their own back gardens, and sometimes they are also made at the local synagogue. Even if you are unable to see the *sukkah* ready for action, you should be able to see the frame of the *sukkah* which is probably re-used each year.

Figure 94

OTHER ROOMS

There will also be additional rooms where the community can meet and celebrate important life rituals such as weddings, and for *Kiddush*, the blessing of wine to mark the opening of *Shabbat*. There will be facilities for parties and for the teaching of Hebrew and for Religious Education.

Possible activities for pupils

1 Make a list of all the things that go on in a synagogue and its buildings, apart from worship.

2 Ask particularly to be shown the kitchen facilities and ask about the Jewish food laws. What rules do you have about food?

3 Make a mezuzah case from a small container and put inside it a small scroll that contains either a prayer or writing which expresses what is important to you in life.

4 Copy the symbols from the curtain covering the Holy Ark and from the mantles on the Torah scrolls. Try to find out more about them from a library.

5 Make a class scroll with your class rules written on it. Put it up in your classroom on display.

6 Make a cover or container for a special book that you want to keep nicely. Think of some appropriate symbols to put on it.

7 On your visit to the synagogue, ask what would happen to the *Ner Tamid* if there was a power cut. What provisions have been made for this?

8 What do we mean when we say that something is or isn't 'written in tablets of stone'?

9 Look up the Ten Commandments in Exodus 20: 1–17. Why do you think they are seen as fundamentally important for human society?

10 Draw the shape of the two tablets of stone, and write on it the laws that you think are most important for our world today.

11 Write a short guide book for other pupils of your age visiting either a liberal, reform or orthodox synagogue.

12 Find out how *Purim* is celebrated within the synagogue and how it is made fun for children.

13 Make a list showing how the synagogue is an extension of the Jewish home; for example, the welcoming of the *Shabbat* Bride on Friday night.

Visiting an Islamic mosque

Introduction

An Islamic place of worship is called a mosque, or *masjid* in Arabic (the language of Islam). Mosque/*masjid* means 'place of prostration' because it is where Muslims prostrate themselves on the ground in humility before God. A mosque does not have to be a building, because Muslims can prostrate themselves in any clean place. In hot, dry countries a mosque could be an open-air courtyard. In a Muslim home, a room can become a mosque for the family prayers. However, if you are taking a class on a visit to a mosque it is likely that you will be visiting a building, either purpose-built or specially converted for the purpose.

The first British mosque was built in Woking in Surrey in 1889 (Figure 95). There are now hundreds of mosques, because Islam is the second largest religion in Great Britain.

Figure 95

Background

Muhammad lived from 570 to 632 CE. He is regarded in Islam as the greatest and final Messenger of Allah. He denounced the idolatry of his time and recalled people to the worship of the One God (Al-lah is Arabic for The God).

Muhammad ruled an Islamic state from the city of Madinah in the last ten years of his life. He built his home where his camel stopped, and the courtyard in the centre of his house became a mosque where people gathered to pray with him. A large, green-domed mosque now stands on this site in Madinah. Muhammad's body is buried there.

What you might see
DOME AND MINARET (FIGURE 96)

Many mosques are built with a traditional dome and minaret, and these are a useful way to recognise a mosque from the outside. Neither of these features is essential, and in fact they are more useful in Islamic countries. The dome allows the air to circulate. The minaret is a tall tower from which the call to prayer is made. In Christendom church bells are rung before a service, but in Islam the human voice alerts Muslims to the prayer times. However, these are not

Figure 96

Figure 97

always used in non-Muslim countries where laws may forbid this as a public disturbance.

PRAYER HALL

There will not be much furniture to see in a mosque because the prayer hall has to have plenty of space for Muslims to go through the prayer movements.

SHOE RACK (FIGURE 98)

Most mosques will have shoe racks or somewhere to leave shoes. Muslims remove their shoes before entering the prayer hall. They do not want to tread dirt indoors where they sit, kneel and place their foreheads on the floor.

Figure 98

WUDU – WASHING FACILITIES (FIGURE 99)

Washing facilities are provided so that Muslims are clean and refreshed for prayer. They must go through a procedure in which they wash their hands, then rinse out their mouth three times, their nose three times and their face three times, then wash their right arm, then the left, then their head, neck and ears, and finally wash their feet thoroughly, starting with the right foot.

Figure 99

CARPETING AND PRAYER MATS (FIGURE 100)

Because Muslims prostrate themselves in prayer, they need a soft floor to kneel on, and mosques are therefore usually carpeted. Many have modern carpets in the design of lots of small prayer mats, so that each Muslim has a space marked out for them to pray. When Muslims arrive for prayer, they fill up each line from the front. Standing shoulder to shoulder emphasises their unity.

Sometimes Muslims put down individual prayer mats on which to pray in a mosque. A prayer mat always has an arch design on it, which is pointed in the correct direction for prayer. Muslims are forbidden to depict any living creatures on their prayer mats or anywhere else in the mosque. This is because Muhammad forbade the worship of idols, and he feared that people would revert to idolatry if they continued to use images. Islamic art has therefore developed in other ways than figurative art, such as intricate geometric patterns. Nor would you see Arabic writing on a prayer mat. Passages from their holy book, the Qur'an, are often used to adorn mosques, but it would be seen as disrespectful to put them on the floor and to stand or kneel on them.

Figure 100

MEN'S AND WOMEN'S AREAS

You will see that some wash and rest areas are for the men and others for women. Similarly, men and women are separated for prayer so that they do not distract each other. There is often a women's balcony or an area sectioned off at the back of the prayer hall for the women. Women can pray here without any worries that the men are looking at them.

MIHRAB (FIGURE 101)

There will be something in the prayer-hall to indicate the *qiblah*, the direction for prayer. It is called the *mihrab* and may be an alcove or niche in a wall, or it could be a piece of furniture (as in the London Central Mosque). The prayer leader, called the *imam*, faces into the *mihrab*, where his voice resonates back into the prayer hall.

Muslims pray in the direction of the *Ka'bah* in the city of Makkah in Saudi Arabia. This is the centre of Islam. The Ka'bah is an empty building which once

Figure 101

housed idols that Muhammad destroyed. It is now a symbol of God who is too great to be depicted in any way, and of the unity of Islam, as Muslims all face inwards towards the same point in prayer. In this photograph of the exterior of Woking Mosque, it is possible to see that the *mihrab* is an integral part of the construction of the building (Figure 102).

Figure 103

Figure 102

MINBAR (FIGURE 103)

This is a raised platform where the *imam* sits to preach the Friday midday sermon. It must be at least three steps high, and in some mosques it is much higher than this. Some are quite plain, whereas others are very ornate. The Friday early afternoon

prayer time is known as the congregational prayers, when all Muslims who can are encouraged to attend. The prayers are followed by a sermon.

CLOCKS (FIGURE 104)

You will usually see clock faces in the entrance of a mosque showing the times of prayer. Muslims must pray five times a day within certain periods of time:

1   between dawn and sunrise;

2   after midday in the early afternoon;

3 late afternoon;

4 just after sunset;

5 at night time, before going to bed.

The clock faces at a mosque show the times when the five daily prayers will take place there. The sixth face shows the time of the second prayer on Friday, followed by a sermon, when Muslims make a special effort to attend. The prayer times will change throughout the year, as the times of sunrise and sunset change.

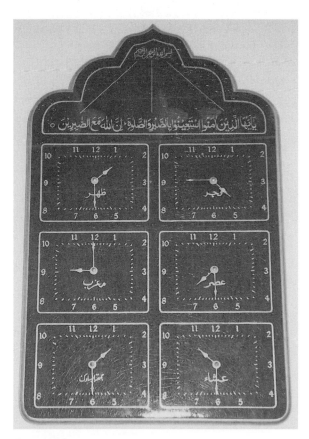

Figure 104

PRAYER BEADS

You may see some prayer beads for people to use if they wish. Some Muslims use these for their private prayers. They are called *subhah*, and the act of using

them is called *tasbih*. They have either ninety nine beads, separated into three sections by three 'rogue' beads; or they have thirty three beads. Worshippers pass each bead through their thumb and forefinger to keep count of their prayers and to concentrate on them. They may use the beads to repeat praises like 'Glory be to Allah' or to remember the ninety nine 'Beautiful Names' by which God is described in the Qur'an (such as 'All-Merciful' and 'All-Compassionate').

QUR'AN (FIGURE 105)

You are likely to see some copies of the Qur'an in the prayer hall for worshippers to read. They will certainly be kept elsewhere in the building. Passages from the Qur'an may also decorate parts of the mosque. The Qur'an is the holy book of Islam. Muslims believe that it contains the words of God passed down through Muhammad. Because it was orginally given in Arabic, they have retained it in this language so that none of its original meaning and beauty is lost. Muslims in non-Arabic speaking countries have to learn Arabic specially in order to read it.

Figure 105

ZAKAH BOX (FIGURE 106)

Zakah is the obligatory annual payment of 2.5 per cent of a Muslim's wealth to the poor. In Islamic countries this is usually collected by the state as a tax. In non-Islamic countries Muslims must make the payment for themselves. You may see a *Zakah* box at the mosque for these donations. You may also see evidence of specific appeals for current issues such as natural disasters in Islamic countries, through organisations such as Islamic Relief.

Figure 107

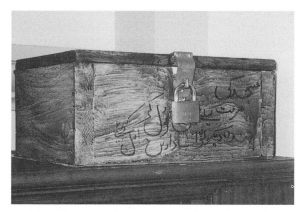

Figure 106

MADRASAH (FIGURES 107 AND 108)

Most mosques in the United Kingdom will have facilities for learning the Qur'an and for basic Islamic teaching within the whole Muslim community. In these photographs some girls can be seen attending a summer school within one of the halls in the grounds of the mosque (Figures 107 and 108).

Figure 108

Possible activities for pupils

1   Draw or make a prayer mat of your own design. Remember that it must have an arch in it, and must not show living creatures. Decorate it with a pattern.

2   Find out some of the 99 beautiful names of Allah and consider what they mean.

3 Try to find out how prayer beads are used in different religions. Why do you think so many religions use them?

4 Ask if there are rooms where Muslim children come to learn to read the Qur'an, and find out more about this school (known as a *madrasah*). Think up some questions to ask, such as:

i) At what age do children start to learn to read the Qur'an?

ii) How is it taught?

iii) How long does it usually take to be able to read it?

iv) What title is given to Muslims who learn the whole Qur'an by heart?

v) Do adults also study the Qur'an?

5 If the mosque is a large one, there is likely to be a library with copies of the Qur'an and also Hadith, which are books containing accounts of what the Prophet Muhammad said and did. There will also be other scholarly Islamic books and journals. Ask to see the library.

6 Interview the *imam* about his role and responsibilities within the Muslim community.

7 Talk with Muslims about some of the issues they face in living in the United Kingdom today.

MOSQUE VISIT GUIDELINES (ISSUED BY A MOSQUE)

- Shoes are to be removed at the reception.

- Complete silence must be observed when prayers are in progress.

- Clothes must be loose, long and non-see through for females, and it is requested that they wear some sort of head covering. No skirts or shorts please. Females should wear trousers. Males also must dress modestly.

- Camera or video recorders are not allowed inside the Masjid (Mosque) without permission.

- Visits can not be made on Fridays, any Islamic Holidays, Bank Holidays or during the month of Ramadan.

TOUR PROGRAMME

1:10 Reception

1:15 Move to gallery. Listen to call to prayer.

1:30 Congregational prayer begins.

1:45 Prayer ends. Tour of Masjid begins.

2:00 Introduction to Islam.

2:05 Questions and Answers.

2:20 Light refreshments.

2:30 Farewell.

Visiting a Hindu mandir

Introduction to Hinduism

Hinduism is the oldest of the world religions and has its roots in the civilisation of the Indus Valley in Northern India from about 3100 BCE. The word 'Hinduism' is in reality a Western term for the many diverse practices emerging from the Indus Valley (hence the name 'Hindu'). Hindus themselves prefer to call their religion *'Sanatana Dharma'*, which is difficult to translate properly into English. Perhaps the nearest translation would be the 'Eternal Righteousness' or 'Eternal Law' or even 'Eternal Way of Life or Religion'.

Most of the Hindu *mandirs* or temples in Britain follow the traditions of Northern rather than Southern India. There is so much variety in Hindu *mandirs* in the United Kingdom that it is difficult to begin to describe them within the context of this book. Having said this, there are some common characteristics, but beware of generalisations. In short, Hindu *mandirs* are all different and full of surprises!

Hinduism is often misunderstood as worshipping more than one God. In reality, Hindus believe that there is One Reality which pervades the universe: Brahman. It is the goal for all Hindus to realise their one-ness with Brahman and therefore their one-ness with the whole cosmos. Hindus believe in reincarnation, and argue that it takes many lifetimes

Figure 109

to achieve this full realisation of Brahman. The images of the Hindu deities that you will see in the *mandir* are regarded as stepping stones to help Hindus to reach a full understanding of Brahman.

Mandirs in the United Kingdom

Hindu *mandirs* in Britain may be purpose-built like the impressive Shri Swaminarayan Temple in Neasden (Figure 109). Often, however, they may be converted buildings such as an old church or house. They may have a variety of names, such as the Shree Sita Ram Temple, the Shree Hindu Mandir, the Sanatan Temple and Community Centre and so on. Most are community centres as well as places of worship and this becomes obvious when visiting them. They are quite busy places and are usually open at all hours.

Hindu families will usually have their own shrine in a room in their homes, so the community function of the *mandir* is an important element.

What you might see

When you enter a *mandir*, there will be a place in the foyer for you to leave your shoes. There will probably be a noticeboard listing some of the activities and concerns of the Hindu community. This can be a useful resource for pupils to study and research.

THE PRAYER HALL

On entering the main prayer hall, there may be a bell which is rung by devotees. This indicates their intention to worship. There is no furniture within the main body of the hall as worshippers will stand or sit. The predominant features within the prayer hall are the *murtis* (images) of the various deities revered

within a particular *mandir*. The most popular deities will be those linked with Vishnu and Shiva. So, for example, those associated with Vishnu include:

Lakshmi	*goddess of wealth and prosperity*
Krishna with his consort, Radha (Figure 110)	*Krishna is an avatar (literally 'coming down') of Vishnu and is 'God revealed' within the Bhagavad Gita*

Figure 110

Rama and Sita (Figure 111)	*Prince Rama is the hero of the epic Ramayana and is also an avatar of Vishnu*

Figure 111

Figure 112

Hanuman	*is not a deity, but a symbol of the perfect devotee of Vishnu in the form of Rama*

Those associated with Shiva include:

Parvati, Durga and Kali (Figure 112)	*The mother goddess. Different forms of the power or 'shakti' of Shiva. Some of these forms are quite fearsome and represent the terrifying and awesome powers needed to destroy the evils of ignorance and selfishness*

Ganesha (Figure 113)	*The son of Shiva, the elephant-headed god who removes obstacles from the path of those who pray to him*

There will be many other deities which are popular within different communities. For example, there may be representations of the different planets, as astrology plays an important function within Hinduism (Figure 114). There may also be an image that represents all the other deities which are not publicly recognised within the *mandir*, so as not to offend them! Hinduism is a very pragmatic religion and this is illustrated by the absence of any image of Brahma, the Creator. He has already done his work

Figure 113

Figure 114

and therefore prayers need not be directed to him any more! This is probably why Ganesha is so popular in *mandirs* and home shrines. As remover of obstacles he has an important role to perform: life is full of potential hazards and pitfalls. (For a more detailed description of the Hindu deities and their symbols, please refer to *Religious Artefacts in the Classroom*, pages 96–112.)

How the deities are revered in worship

People will bring offerings of money, food, flowers and so on to the *mandir*. These will often be left for the Brahmin priest when he leads the *puja* (worship) (Figure 115). The deities are revered by being washed with water or yoghurt. They may be dressed with fine cloth or with garlands of flowers and other decorations (Figure 116).

Figure 115

The Brahmin can be heard chanting in Sanskrit, the ancient sacred language of Hinduism, using prayers from the Vedas, the most important sacred writings of the Hindu religion. Devotees will come and stand before the image of the deity and say prayers silently or aloud. They may adopt a variety of

Figure 116

their hands over the flame when it is offered to them and symbolically draw the warmth and light of the flame to their faces. This represents an internalising of God's purity and energy within the heart of each devotee.

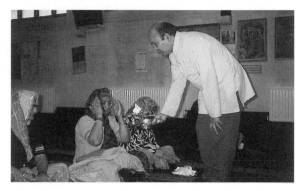

Figure 117

PUJA TRAY (FIGURE 118)

Within the *mandir* and indeed within most Hindu homes you will find a *puja* tray. This consists of a tray made of metal and contains five elements to represent the fact that all five senses are fully involved in Hindu worship or *puja*.

postures, some even prostrating themselves fully in front of the image, but usually standing in quiet recollection. Where there are many deities represented, *puja* may consist of a journey from *murti* to *murti*, depending upon the individual and seasonal festivals.

ARTI (FIGURE 117)

The *arti* ceremony is celebrated at various points throughout the day. It is a ceremony where a special lamp known as an *arti* lamp is lit. It has five cotton-bud wicks, which are soaked in ghee. When lit, it makes one very bright flame and this is taken around the *mandir* by the Brahmin and offered to the *murti* and then to the devotees. Each person will place

Figure 118

On the tray you will see:

a bell	*This is rung at the beginning of* puja *to alert the deity that worship is about to commence. (Sense: hearing)*
incense holder	*Incense is burnt to create a pleasing aroma for the deity. (Sense: smell)*
arti *or* diva *lamp*	*For lighting and burning throughout* puja. *(Sense: sight)*
container for sandal paste	*The paste is used to mark the forehead of the devotee. This is known as a* tilak *mark and is a sign of God's blessing. (Sense: touch)*
a water pot and spoon	*Contains water, or milk/yoghurt and represents cleansing and purification. It is offered to the deity and to the devotee. (Sense: taste)*

On the tray there will also be offerings of fruit, nuts, sweets, flowers, milk, rice and so on.

Symbols

The most common symbols you will see within the *mandir* are Aum and the swastika.

AUM (FIGURE 119)

Aum is the main symbol which has been adopted for Hinduism within the United Kingdom. It is an ancient symbol and represents the sacred syllable or first sound which brought about the whole of creation. It

Figure 119

is also used as a mantra or chant in order to aid meditation in yoga. In birth ceremonies the symbol Aum is traced on to the newborn baby's tongue with honey.

THE SWASTIKA (FIGURE 120)

The *swastika* is also an ancient symbol and represents the wheel of *samsara*: the Hindu belief that we are locked into a continual cycle of rebirth until we are able to grasp fully the reality of Brahman. This realisation leads to *moksha* (release from the fetters of rebirth) and is the goal for all Hindus. The swastika, as we know, was taken by the Nazis and distorted into the crooked cross. Hindus are dismayed that their sacred symbol has been perverted in such a way. Some pupils will see this symbol and make the wrong connections, so teachers will need to be both proactive and sensitive.

Figure 120

SHIVA LINGA (FIGURE 121)

Most *mandirs* which honour Shiva will have a Shiva Linga. This is a phallic symbol which represents the creative energy of Shiva. It is so subtle, however, that pupils will not realise its significance. You will notice that in some *mandirs*, it is quite a prominent feature. It is bathed in milk and yoghurt and adorned with flowers and offerings from the *puja* tray. There is a story about the Shiva Linga which is more appropriate for younger children within the artefacts book (pages 104–5).

Figure 121

Prashad

Hospitality is an important aspect of Hindu society, so you may be offered a midday meal of rice and vegetable curry. This can be negotiated before the visit. As you are leaving the *mandir*, you may well be offered food, such as fruit or nuts to take with you. This food is called *Prashad* and has been blessed and offered to the deities. It is polite to accept all gifts. They need not be consumed there and then. Some parents may feel uneasy about their children consuming food which has been offered to Hindu deities, so you will need to be aware of this.

Case study: the Shree Gannapatha Temple in Wimbledon (Figure 122)

This *mandir* is particularly interesting because attached to it is an interfaith prayer hall. From the outside, it is possible to see that this Hindu place of worship was once a Presbyterian chapel. Notice the sign on the outside (Figure 123), which contains the symbols of some of the main world religions. This is not typical of *mandirs* but indicates the presence of an interfaith group based on the teachings of Sai Baba, a world renowned Hindu guru (teacher).

On entering the *mandir*, you will see much of what is described above within the main prayer hall. An interesting addition, however, is the telephone within the main body of the prayer hall. During visits I have made, it is not unusual for the telephone to ring while the Brahmin is performing *puja*. He simply stops what he is doing, answers the phone and then returns to his religious duties. At first I was quite surprised until I realised that for Hindus, religion and life are not separate entities. They do not compartmentalise things in the way that we tend to do in the West. It would be interesting to consider the impact of a telephone within a church service, especially during the sermon!

There is also a kitchen for communal meals, as this building is very much a focal point for the Hindu community in this area of south London.

Walking from the main prayer hall, which is both busy and full of images of the deities, you enter the

Figure 122

Figure 123

Figure 124

interfaith prayer hall and there is a completely different atmosphere. There is a feeling of space and a tangible sense of contemplation. There is one focal point within the *mandir* and this is a raised dais with

a life-size statue of the previous incarnation of Sai Baba (Figure 124). There is a beautiful, ornate, empty chair and a large, garlanded photograph of Sai Baba's feet. Sai Baba taught that all religions are but different paths to the same reality. Services here, therefore, are attended by people from all religious backgrounds and the hymns that they sing are drawn from a variety of sources and reflect this belief in the validity of all religions in the quest for truth. Around the walls are photos of Sai Baba and articles about his teachings and miracles.

Possible activities for pupils

1   Research about the different deities, with particular emphasis on their associated symbols and their significance.

2   Ask a Hindu:

  – what is their favourite deity and why?

  – what is their understanding of Brahman?

  – what they do when they attend the *mandir*, or when they perform *puja* in their homes?

3   Find out what takes place when a Hindu baby is born, or at a Hindu wedding.

4   Draw and label the different elements of a *puja* tray, indicating how each of the five senses are involved in Hindu worship.

5   Find out how Ganesha received his elephant head and why he is so popular in Hindu devotion.

6   Invite a Hindu dance troup to visit the school.

7   Look at short extracts from the Bhagavad Gita on devotion to Krishna or the concept of Brahman within the Upanishads.

Visiting a Buddhist vihara

Background

Buddhism goes back about 2,500 years to its founder Siddharta Gautama. Prince Siddhartha was born a Hindu, within a wealthy family in Northern India. When he was born, his father, who was a king, was informed by a holy man that his son would become a great religious teacher. His father was determined that Siddhartha should succeed him on the throne and decided to prevent him from experiencing anything which would aid the fulfilment of the prophecy. He kept Siddhartha within the confines of the palace grounds and ensured that he did not come into contact with anything which might lead him to question the meaning of life. He even provided his son with a beautiful wife.

However, one day Siddhartha secretly left the palace with his trusted servant. On the journey he saw four things which deeply troubled him: an old man, a sick man, a dead man and a holy man. He had never seen any suffering before and the holy man seemed to be contented even though he had no possessions. He questioned his servant and discovered that suffering, illness, old age and death came to all people. That

night he set off to seek out an answer to what he had seen that day (Figure 125).

After meeting a group of five Hindu ascetics in the forest, he tried to share their way of life and nearly died from his ascetic practices. He then set off on his own until he came to the village of Bodh Gaya. Here he sat under a tree, determined to meditate until he discovered a reason for suffering in the world. Under this tree, which is now known as the Bodhi tree (tree of enlightenment or wisdom), he eventually understood the cause of suffering and how it could be prevented. This realisation is known as the enlightenment, and from then on Siddhartha became known as the Buddha, the enlightened one. His first disciples were the five ascetics he had met in the forest. He spent the rest of his life living as a monk and preaching throughout India. His teachings are found within the Four Noble Truths and within the Eightfold Path. This path is described as the Middle Way as it avoids the extremes of the luxurious life he experienced as a child and the ascetic life he tried out in the forest before his enlightenment. You can read more about the teachings of the Buddha in any good book on Buddhism.

The spread of Buddhism

Buddhism spread throughout the world and is now found in a variety of forms. The two main groups are Theravada and Mahayana.

Theravada Buddhism, or Way of the Elders, is also known as the Southern Transmission, as it is mainly found within the countries of South Asia: Sri Lanka, Myanmar, Laos, Cambodia and Thailand. It focuses mainly on the historical Buddha and emphasises the need for the individual to seek his or her own enlightenment.

Figure 125

Mahayana Buddhism is also called the Northern Transmission, as it came via the northern silk trade route, reaching the northern countries of China, Japan, Vietnam, Korea and Tibet. The main emphasis in Mahayana Buddhism is on the ideal of the Bodhisattva: enlightened beings who, having reached nirvana, aid others to do the same. Bodhisattvas live in a realm of permanent transcendence where they work for the salvation of others.

Buddhism in the United Kingdom

To date, there are about 120 Buddhist *viharas*, temples or centres within the United Kingdom, and many more places where Buddhist groups meet, such as in private homes or in hired halls. There is a great deal of variety within these groups and most Buddhist traditions are represented in some form within Great Britain.

Buddhist *viharas*

A Buddhist place of worship can have a variety of names. Strictly speaking the word '*vihara*' indicates that there is not just a shrine for Buddhist devotions, but there is also a monastery where Buddhist monks or nuns live. The place of worship may also be called a temple or even a centre.

What you might see
THE SHRINE ROOM (FIGURE 127)

The focal point of any Buddhist *vihara* is the shrine room. Buddhist devotion is called *puja* and may contain the following elements:

• devotion to an image of the Buddha (*Buddharupa*)

• readings from the sacred scriptures

• chanting

Figure 126

Figure 127

The shrine room may also be used for meditation, or there may be a separate room for this. *Puja* can also take place at home.

BUDDHA IMAGES (FIGURE 128)

The shrine room will contain an image or images of the Buddha. These Buddha images (*Buddharupas*) will be in different forms representing different aspects of the Buddha's enlightenment, or generally characteristics of the enlightened mind. These different representations of the Buddha image also reflect the different concerns of Mahayana and Theravada Buddhism. However, both traditions use *mudras* (hand gestures) as an artistic device in order to convey Buddhist teaching. The use of *mudras* has its origin in Hindu iconography and dance.

The five most popular *mudras* used in Buddhist art are:

Bhumisparsa-mudra *This means the 'earth-touching' Buddha. On receiving enlightenment, the Buddha called upon the earth to witness this event.*

Varada-mudra *This representation shows compassion and giving.*

Dhyana-mudra *This represents total concentration in meditation.*

Abhaya-mudra   *The upraised palm signifies protection and reassurance. The left hand remains in the dhyana-mudra.*

4

Vitarka-mudra   *This depicts the teaching of Buddhist doctrine and reasoning.*

5

Other symbols that you may see associated with Buddha images might include:

* the *lotus flower*   In Buddhism, the lotus flower is a symbol of enlightenment. This beautiful flower emerges from the muddy waters of the pond – all clean and pure. Like the lotus, the human mind is able to rise up, out of the mud of selfishness and ignorance, to the sunlight of enlightenment. The Buddha image may be shown holding a lotus blossom, or may be sitting on a lotus throne.

* the *flame*   Some images of the historical Buddha (Sakyamuni) show him with a flame emerging from the top of his head. This shows that he has reached enlightenment (Figure 129).

* The *vajra (diamond or thunderbolt)*   Sometimes the Buddha image will be holding a *vajra*. This is sometimes referred to as the 'diamond thunderbolt' or 'diamond sceptre'. It represents the need for resolve and determination in the quest for enlightenment. *For further information on different Buddha images and Buddhist iconography,*

Figure 129

Figure 130

Figure 131

see *pages 115–20 of* Religious artefacts in the Classroom (Figure 130).

OFFERING BOWLS

You may see seven bowls containing water in front of the Buddha image. These offerings are a way of expressing devotion to the Buddha. Although '*puja*' is the Sanskrit word for 'worship', 'devotion' is a better translation for most Buddhists, as *puja* is performed to aid the spiritual development of the individual rather than to seek the help of a deity. In many ways the offering bowls show that the Buddha is being treated as a guest of honour, who would be offered water for washing and refreshment after a long journey.

OTHER OFFERINGS (FIGURE 131)

You will often see offerings of flowers and candles and incense in front of the Buddha image. Each of

these offerings shows that life is transient: that everything is subject to change. For example, the fresh flowers continue to grow and eventually begin to wither and die. This acts as a visible and constant reminder to Buddhists of the reality of impermanence. The candle represents the light of Buddha's teachings, which in turn bring enlightenment. The incense represents the sweet fragrance of the Buddha's teachings.

BELL OR GONG

This is used to alert people to the next stage of meditation or *puja*.

CUSHIONS

These are simply there for making meditation as comfortable as possible. Sometimes they may be set out in long rows on either side of the shrine room. If there is a *vihara*, these may be reserved for the monks within the community.

THANKAS

A *thanka* is a cloth wall-hanging which is popular in Tibet and Bhutan. You may find these on the walls of some Buddhist shrines. They can be used as an aid to meditation and may depict images such as a mandala or the 'Wheel of Life'. For more information on *thankas*, mandalas and the 'Wheel of Life', see pages 121–5 of *Religious Artefacts in the Classroom*.

Case study: the Buddhapadipa Temple in Wimbledon (Figure 132)

The Buddhapadipa Temple is a purpose-built Thai temple nestling hidden in the suburbs of Wimbledon in south London. It is a *vihara*, as a community of Thai monks are now well established in the large house which existed long before the temple was built (Figure 133). People from all walks of life,

Figure 132

Figure 133

whatever their creed, come from far afield, just to enjoy the peace and tranquillity of the temple grounds. You do not have to be a Buddhist to appreciate the magnificent craftsmanship and vision which has gone into the creation of this oasis at the heart of London's suburbs (Figure 134).

A series of walks and areas for meditation have been created within the temple grounds, which incorporate ponds, bridges and ornamental features. This creates the feeling that there is a harmony between Buddhist teaching and the natural environment.

The temple itself is crafted by Thai builders using traditional Thai architecture and building methods. The finished result is exquisite, with a mixture of white, gold and red paintwork. Recently a series of small classrooms have been erected for the many visitors who come to the *vihara* (Figure 135).

Inside the temple is the shrine room with a traditional Thai Buddharupa as the main focal point. Raised platforms have been constructed on either side of the shrine room for the monks to sit during *puja* and meditation. One of the most striking features of the shrine room is the artwork which covers all the walls and the ceilings. These masterpieces were painted by Thai artists who spent years in their creation. They depict scenes from the life of Siddharta Gautama and even include cameos of Charlie Chaplin and Margaret Thatcher!

Downstairs, there are separate meditation rooms as the *vihara* is a popular place for people to learn about the Buddhist way of life and meditation techniques.

Figure 134

Figure 136

Figure 135

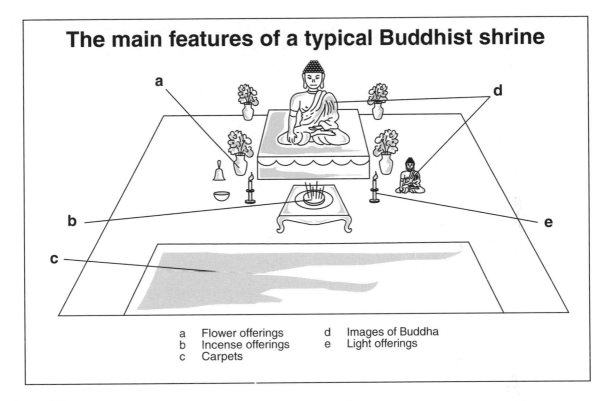

The main features of a typical Buddhist shrine

a	Flower offerings	d	Images of Buddha
b	Incense offerings	e	Light offerings
c	Carpets		

Figure 137

Possible activities for pupils

1 Ask pupils to find out about the following:

– the Four Noble Truths;

– the Eightfold Path;

– the Three Refuges;

– the Five Precepts;

and consider these with regard to their own experiences and values.

2 Pupils could dramatise some of the key moments in the life of Siddhartha Gautama leading up to his eventual enlightenment under the Bodhi tree.

3 They could consider their own experiences of suffering and of suffering within the world, and explore their own views as to why suffering exists.

4 Interview a Buddhist monk about their daily life and why they became a monk. Ask them to teach the group some basic techniques in meditation. Consider whether we need times of stillness in a busy society.

5 Look at a variety of Buddha images and determine which *mudras* they use and what each represents.

6 Older pupils could find a poster of the Wheel of Life and explore the symbols within it.

7 Research into the life and exile of the Dalai Lama and his importance for Tibetan and other Buddhists today.

Visiting a Sikh gurdwara

Background

Sikhism is the youngest of the great world religions. It was founded by Guru Nanak (1469–1539) and was an attempt to bring together Hindus and Muslims in the Punjab region of Northern India. Guru Nanak saw all religions as striving towards the One Truth and the worship of One God. This attempt at bringing the two religions together failed, however, and the new religion of Sikhism was born.

Guru Nanak taught that the One God (Sat Nam, literally, 'True Name') was more interested in people's actions than simply beliefs. He taught that all men and women are brothers and sisters and should enjoy equality in all aspects of life.

Guru Nanak was followed by a further nine gurus (literally, 'teachers'), the last being Guru Gobind Singh. It was he who instigated the brotherhood of Sikhs, the Khalsa, and the five signs of being a Sikh: the five Ks. These are:

Kesh	*uncut hair*
Kangha	*comb*
Kirpan	*sword*
Kara	*bracelet*
Kachera	*shorts/under-garments*

You can read all about the five Ks and their significance on pages 132–4 of Religious Artefacts in the Classroom.

Figure 138

Guru Gobind Singh revealed that there would be no more human gurus after himself and the Sikhs should look to their sacred book, the Guru Granth Sahib, as their eternal living guru.

Visiting a *gurdwara*
INTRODUCTION

Gurdwara means literally 'Gateway to the Guru' as it contains the Guru Granth Sahib, the teachings of the Ten Gurus. It is also unique in the fact that it contains extracts from the teachings of Hindu and Muslim saints.

Gurdwaras in the United Kingdom may be purpose built. Often some of the oldest *gurdwaras* are buildings which have been converted by the Sikh community, such as an old bakery, an employment office and so on. They will have names such as the Tooting Khalsa Centre, the Guru Nanak Community Centre, Guru Har Rai Gurdwara, Gurdwara Singh Sabha and so on (Figure 138).

Figure 139

OUTSIDE THE GURDWARA

Before entering the *gurdwara* look out for the saffron-coloured flag with the Khanda symbol upon it (see Khanda below). This flag is called the Nishan Sahib (Figure 139) and is renewed during the annual festival of *Baisakhi*. This is an important festival, when Sikhs will remember how Guru Gobind Singh founded the Khalsa (Sikh brotherhood) in 1699.

The story tells how 20,000 Sikhs were gathered to celebrate the festival of *Baisakhi*. Guru Gobind Singh appeared in front of the Sikh crowd brandishing a sword and cried out: 'I need a Sikh who is willing to give his life to God and to the Guru.' After moments of disbelief and murmuring, one Sikh stood up and offered his life to the Guru. They both stepped into a tent, and the crowd gasped when they heard the swish of the sword and the clump of a head falling to the floor. The Guru came out of the tent with his sword dripping in blood and demanded another volunteer to step forward. This took place five times and the crowd were becoming extremely agitated, thinking that the Guru had gone mad. However, after the fifth man had gone into the tent, the Guru reappeared together with the five brave Sikhs alive and smiling. It was a test by Guru Gobind Singh to see who was worthy of forming the core of the Khalsa, the leaders of the new Sikh community.

After this, Guru Gobind Singh gave the Sikhs the five Ks to mark their new identity. *Baisakhi*, therefore is a significant festival which will be marked in many *gurdwaras* by focusing on the five Ks and by the Amrit ceremony, which is a form of initiation into the Khalsa. *(For more information on this see page 136 of* Religious Artefacts in the Classroom.*)*

THE FOYER

On entering a *gurdwara*, males and females should cover their heads and remove their shoes. There is usually shelving for the shoes (Figure 140) and spare head coverings for visitors. You may also be asked to wash your hands.

Figure 141

over it (Figure 141). Under the canopy the sacred book, the Guru Granth Sahib, is kept on a raised cushion. When Sikhs arrive for personal or corporate worship, they will walk up the central carpet and prostrate themselves before the sacred writings (Figure 142). They will place offerings of money or food in front of the dais and then find a place to sit facing the Guru Granth Sahib. (*Note:* Sometimes visitors may be expected to bow before the Guru Granth Sahib. It will be important to explain to whoever shows your group around that for non-Sikhs to do this, would not be in keeping with the aims of an educational visit.)

Figure 140

PRAYER HALL

On entering the prayer room, you will notice the absence of any furniture – it is a simple prayer hall with space for the faithful to sit on the floor. Males sit on one side and females on the other. All face towards a raised dais (*takht*) with a canopy or *palki*

Figure 142

The Guru Granth Sahib is a large book, written in Punjabi, and it is treated as a living guru. When it is not read it is covered with *romalla* cloths which are donated by members of the community. These may be plain or have Sikh emblems on them such as the *Ik Onkar* or the *Khanda* (see below).

When the Guru Granth Sahib is opened it is treated with the greatest respect. It is considered disrespectful to turn one's back to it. A person known as the Granthi will sit cross-legged in front of the book. He will wave an object called a *chauri* (Figure 143) over the book to show the sacred nature of the Guru Granth Sahib. The *chauri* is usually made of yak's hair attached to a wooden or metal handle. Both the *romalla* cloths and the waving of the *chauri* show that the Guru Granth Sahib is treated as a living guru.

Figure 143

The Granthi is someone who is respected within the community. His role is to read and interpret the Guru Granth Sahib during Sikh worship.

MUSIC

Music is an important element of Sikh worship. Hymns from the Guru Granth Sahib known as *shabads* are led by accomplished Sikh musicians.

Sometimes when you visit a *gurdwara* it may be possible to arrange for musicians to play to the pupils. Traditional instruments are usually a harmonium and *tablas* (drums) for percussion (Figure 144).

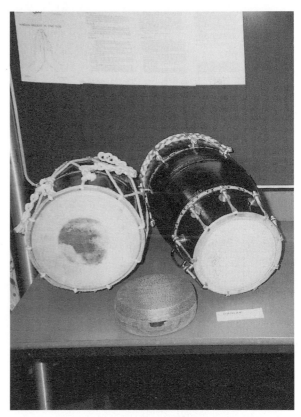

Figure 144

PICTURES OF THE GURUS (FIGURE 145)

Throughout the *gurdwara*, the walls will be decorated with pictures of Guru Nanak, Guru Gobind Singh and the other eight gurus. (For more information on these gurus, see pages 134–5 of *Religious Artefacts in the Classroom*.)

Often these pictures are decorated with garlands of tinsel, and pupils will comment that it looks as if it is always Christmas in the *gurdwara*!

Figure 145

Figure 146

SYMBOLS TO LOOK OUT FOR

The Khanda *(Figure 147) This is the main Sikh symbol and is actually made up of three symbols:*

- the double edged sword (*Khanda*), which is used in the *Amrit* or initiation ceremony;

- the circle (*Chakkar*) represents infinity because a circle has no beginning and no end. It points Sikhs to the One God who is timeless and absolute. The circle is also a symbol of restraint and reminds Sikhs to remain within the will of God;

- the two swords (*Kirpan*) represent two types of power and authority. One represents *Peeri* (spiritual power) and the other *Meeri* (earthly/political power).

Figure 147

Ik Onkar *(Figure 148) This symbol forms the opening words of the Mool Mantra which appears at the beginning of every chapter in the Guru Granth Sahib. It means 'There is only one God'.*

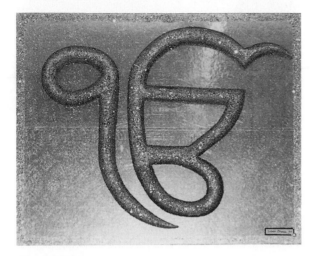

Figure 148

The Mool Mantra *states:*

There is only one God

Truth is his name

He is the creator

He is without fear

He is without hate

He is timeless and without form

He is beyond death, the enlightened one

He can be known by the Guru's grace.

THE GOLDEN TEMPLE (FIGURE 149)

You may also see pictures on the wall of the Golden Temple of Amritsar. This is an exquisite building and is an important site for Sikhs all over the world.

Figure 149

Guru Arjan built the first *gurdwara* at Amritsar, although the Golden Temple itself was not built until about 1801.

The Guru's room

Within every *gurdwara* there is a room where the Guru Granth Sahib is placed when it is not being read. It is usually a small and simple room with a bed on which the sacred book is placed and covered up for the night. Again, this symbolic action shows that the Guru Granth Sahib is treated as a living guru.

Langar (Figures 150 and 151)

Within the *gurdwara* there is a kitchen and dining area called a *langar*. This place for the cooking and serving of communal meals is an important statement in Sikh religion. In India, the caste system prevents different social groups from mixing, including eating together. The *langar* was established by Guru Nanak to show that people, whatever their race, religion, caste, social class or gender, are equal in the eyes of God and within the Sikh community.

When you visit a *gurdwara* you will be offered food in the *langar*. The food is vegetarian and mildly spicy. You will also be offered *Kara Prashad*, blessed food during your visit to the prayer hall (Figure 152). This

Figure 151

is a sweet food made from flour, sugar, water and ghee. *Kara Prashad* should be received with both hands cupped and right hand uppermost. If you feel

Figure 150

Figure 152

Plan of a gurdwara

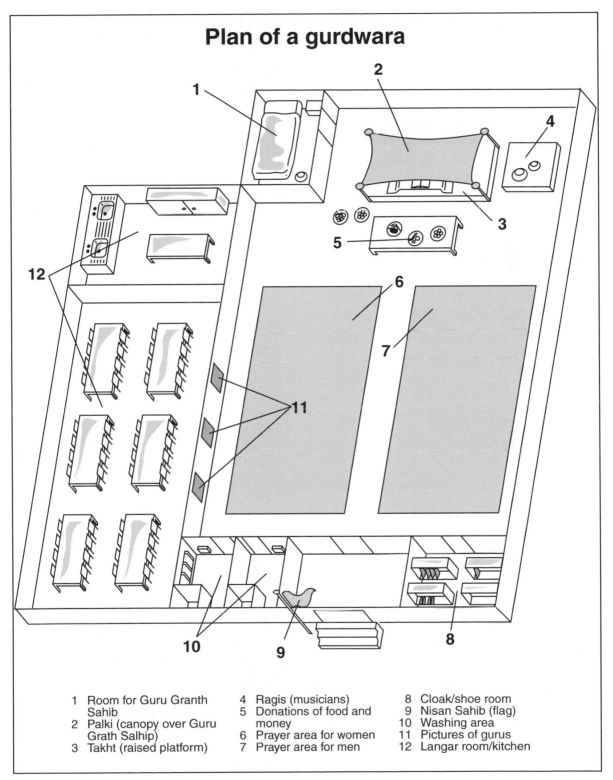

1 Room for Guru Granth Sahib
2 Palki (canopy over Guru Grath Salhip)
3 Takht (raised platform)
4 Ragis (musicians)
5 Donations of food and money
6 Prayer area for women
7 Prayer area for men
8 Cloak/shoe room
9 Nisan Sahib (flag)
10 Washing area
11 Pictures of gurus
12 Langar room/kitchen

Figure 153

unable to receive blessed food, then simply say 'No, thank you' to whoever offers it to you. If possible, explain at the beginning of the visit that you are not being disrespectful in refusing *Kara Prashad*, but following your own religious traditions.

Possible activities for pupils

1 Consider uniforms which pupils may wear to show they belong to a particular group or organisation.

2 Look at the five Ks and explore what each signifies.

3 Interview a Sikh about what wearing the five Ks means to them and some of the issues they face, living in the United Kingdom today.

4 Act out the story of the founding of the Khalsa by Guru Gobind Singh.

5 Ask the Granthi to read some passages of the Guru Granth Sahib.

6 Explore the importance of shared meals within their own lives and within Sikh religion.

7 Make a model of the *gurdwara*, remembering to include key features such as the *takht*, *palki* and Guru Granth Sahib, the *langar* and important symbols.

8 Make and eat *Kara Prashad*. *(You can find the recipe on page 137 of* Religious Artefacts in the Classroom.*)*

9 Find a copy of a Nit Nem (Sikh hymn book) with English translation and explore Sikh beliefs about God through a study of the lyrics.

10 Listen to Sikh music, either at the *gurdwara* or on tape/CD.

Further reading

Religions in the UK
A multi-faith directory
Edited by Paul Weller
University of Derby
ISBN 0 901437 68 9
(Essential directory for any professional who is serious about visiting places of worship and building good relationships with local faith communities. Costly at about £28.00, but invaluable)

Religious Artefacts in the Classroom
Paul Gateshill and Jan Thompson
Hodder & Stoughton
ISBN 0 340 57002 4
(Handbook for teachers KS1–4)

KeyStones Series
Buddhist Vihara
Hindu Mandir, etc
Various authors
A and C Black, London
ISBN various, e.g. 0 7136 4834 1
(KS2 pupils, but a useful introduction for non-specialists)

Places of Worship
Lynne Broadbent and Jan Thompson
Folens Copymaster
ISBN 1 85276309 4
(Open-ended photocopiable materials for Primary and Secondary use)

Christian Buildings
Edited by Brenda Lealman
Christian Education Movement
ISBN 1 85100 009 7

The Christian Faith and its Symbols
Jan Thompson
Hodder & Stoughton
ISBN 0 340 66379 0
(KS3 pupils, but excellent introduction for teachers)

Health and Safety of Pupils on Educational Visits DfEE
An essential guide to good practice

Where we worship series Published by Franklin Watts
Excellent for KS 1–2 pupils
Various authors
ISBN 07496 3153 8 and others

Places of worship
Staffordshire County Council. Available from Four Shires Project, Quality Learning Services, Kingston Centre, Harrowby Street, Stafford ST16 3TU
Activity packs for KS 1–2 pupils

What's special to me?
Religious Buildings
Excellent book for KS1 pupils
Published by Wayland
ISBN 0 7502 2245X

Discovering Churches
Published by Lion
Author: Lois Rock
ISBN 0 7459 2920 6
Suitable for KS3. A teacher's guide is also available

Visiting Churches, Primary RE series
Bromley Education available from Standards and Effectiveness Services, Education Development Centre, Church Lane, Princes Plain, Bromley BR2 8LD
Tel: 0181 462 8911
A teacher's handbook for KS 1–2

Internet sites

There are now many web sites for faith communities throughout the United Kingdom and indeed the world. Some of these have 'virtual visits' to their places the worship, which are useful resources for pupils. Many cathedrals now have their own web sites. Visit RE's own search engine *theresite.org.uk* and be prepared for some serious surfing!

Index